D1326221

Library of
Woodbrooke College,
Selly Oak,
Birmingham.

THE CAMBRIDGE BIBLE COMMENTARY

NEW ENGLISH BIBLE

GENERAL EDITORS

P. R. ACKROYD, A. R. C. LEANEY, J. W. PACKER

I & II CORINTHIANS

THE
FIRST AND SECOND
LETTERS OF PAUL
TO THE
CORINTHIANS

COMMENTARY BY

MARGARET E. THRALL

*Lecturer in Biblical Studies, University College of
North Wales, Bangor*

CAMBRIDGE
AT THE UNIVERSITY PRESS
1965

PUBLISHED BY
THE SYNDICS OF THE CAMBRIDGE UNIVERSITY PRESS

Bentley House, 200 Euston Road, London, N.W. 1
American Branch: 32 East 57th Street, New York, N.Y. 10022
West African Office: P.O. Box 33, Ibadan, Nigeria

©

CAMBRIDGE UNIVERSITY PRESS

1965

227.2

Printed in Great Britain at the University Printing House, Cambridge
(Brooke Crutchley, University Printer)

GENERAL EDITORS' PREFACE

The aim of this series is to provide the text of the New English Bible closely linked to a commentary in which the results of modern scholarship are made available to the general reader. Teachers and young people preparing for such examinations as the General Certificate of Education at Ordinary or Advanced Level in Britain, and similar qualifications elsewhere have been especially kept in mind. The commentators have been asked to assume no specialized theological knowledge, and no knowledge of Greek and Hebrew. Bare references to other literature and multiple references to other parts of the Bible have been avoided. Actual quotations have been given as often as possible.

Within these quite severe limits each commentator will attempt to set out the main findings of recent New Testament scholarship, and to describe the historical background to the text. The main theological content of the New Testament will also be critically discussed.

Much attention has been given to the form of the volumes. The aim is to produce books each of which will be read consecutively from first to last page. The introductory material leads naturally into the text, which itself leads into the alternating sections of commentary. By this means it is hoped that each book will be easily read and remain in the mind as a unity.

The series will be prefaced by a volume—*Understanding the New Testament*—which will outline the larger historical background, say something about the growth and transmission of the text, and answer the question 'Why should we study the New Testament?' Another volume—*The New Testament Illustrated*—will contain maps, diagrams and photographs.

P.R.A.
A.R.C.L.
J.W.P.

EDITOR'S PREFACE

I should like to thank the General Editors for all the useful advice and criticism I received while I was writing this commentary.

M.E.T.

CONTENTS

Map   *page* viii

✳ ✳ ✳ ✳ ✳ ✳ ✳ ✳ ✳ ✳ ✳ ✳ ✳

Corinth and the founding of the Corinthian church   1

Paul's correspondence with the Corinthians   3

The date and place of composition   10

✳ ✳ ✳ ✳ ✳ ✳ ✳ ✳ ✳ ✳ ✳ ✳ ✳

The First Letter of Paul to the Corinthians   14

Unity and Order in the Church   14

The Christian in a Pagan Society   50

Spiritual Gifts   85

Life after Death   102

Christian Giving   115

✳ ✳ ✳ ✳ ✳ ✳ ✳ ✳ ✳ ✳ ✳ ✳ ✳

The Second Letter of Paul to the Corinthians   119

Events following the writing of 1 Corinthians   119

✳ ✳ ✳ ✳ ✳ ✳ ✳ ✳ ✳ ✳ ✳ ✳ ✳

Personal Religion and the Ministry   121

Problems of Church Life and Discipline   155

Trials of a Christian Missionary   166

✳ ✳ ✳ ✳ ✳ ✳ ✳ ✳ ✳ ✳ ✳ ✳ ✳

The Corinthian letters today   183

✳ ✳ ✳ ✳ ✳ ✳ ✳ ✳ ✳ ✳ ✳ ✳ ✳

INDEX   195

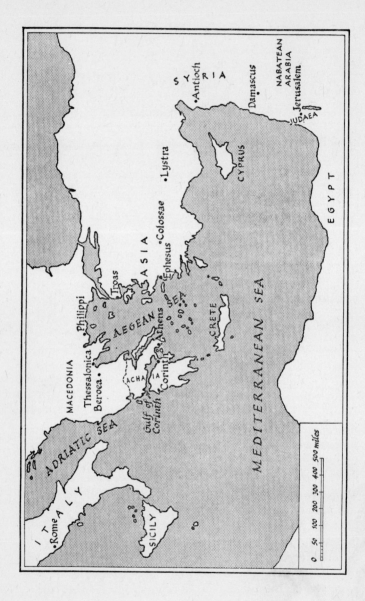

THE MEDITERRANEAN WORLD IN THE TIME OF PAUL

THE
FIRST AND SECOND LETTERS
OF PAUL TO THE
CORINTHIANS

✳ ✳ ✳ ✳ ✳ ✳ ✳ ✳ ✳ ✳ ✳ ✳ ✳

CORINTH AND THE FOUNDING OF THE
CORINTHIAN CHURCH

In the course of his second expedition as a Christian missionary Paul travelled as far as Macedonia and Greece. He paid successful visits to Philippi and Thessalonica (Acts 16: 11 — 17: 4), and then had a less effective encounter with the Athenians (Acts 17: 16–34). Finally he came to Corinth, and stayed there for about two years (Acts 18: 1–18).

Corinth was an important city. In the year 46 B.C. it had been founded as a Roman colony by Julius Caesar, and it was built upon the site of an older Greek city which had been destroyed by the Romans a hundred years earlier. Very little remains of the older city today, except for a ruined temple of Apollo, but the paved streets and main square and the public water fountain which belong to the time of Paul provide a substantial picture of the layout of the city as he knew it. In the first century A.D. it was the capital of the Roman province of Achaia and the place of residence of the proconsul, who administered the affairs of the province on behalf of the Emperor. The view from the steep hill of Acrocorinth which overlooks the ruins suggests another reason for the city's importance. From the summit one can look down on the one side to the waters of the Gulf of Corinth and on the other to the Aegean Sea. The isthmus of Corinth stands between the

I

Adriatic Sea and the Aegean, and lies on the direct route between Italy and Asia Minor. Merchants in the first century who were carrying their goods by sea from west to east or east to west were eager to avoid the long and dangerous journey round the Greek peninsula. They preferred to sail to the isthmus of Corinth and then to take their cargoes overland and transfer them to another boat on the opposite side. This central position on a major trade route brought great commercial prosperity to the city. It also meant that it had a very mixed population. Social conditions in Corinth were notable on two counts. First, although the city was wealthy its wealth was distributed unevenly, and the gap between rich and poor grew steadily wider. Secondly, the Corinthians were notorious for their sexual immorality. Greek slang had turned the name of the city into a verb meaning 'to fornicate' (*korinthiazesthai*). Religion was as mixed as the population. The Roman gods were worshipped, but there were in addition innumerable other cults which had been introduced into Corinth from all parts of the Mediterranean world. There was also a community of Jews in the city, who had their own synagogue.

Paul probably arrived there in the year A.D. 50. We are told in Acts that he became friendly with a Jewish Christian, Aquila by name, and his wife, Priscilla, who had recently left Rome because of the edict of expulsion which the Emperor Claudius had passed against the Jews. This edict came into force in A.D. 49. Paul made his home with Aquila and Priscilla, and began his missionary work by holding discussions in the Jewish synagogue. He converted one of the synagogue officials, a man called Crispus, but since most of the Jews adopted a hostile attitude towards him he gave up teaching in the synagogue and concentrated on preaching to the non-Jewish population. There he met with a considerable degree of success. The Jews tried to make trouble for him by dragging him into court before Gallio, the Roman proconsul, and accusing him of illegal conduct. Gallio, however, took the line that this was a purely religious dispute and nothing to do

with the Roman administration. Paul stayed in Corinth for
some time afterwards and then returned to his headquarters
at Antioch.

PAUL'S CORRESPONDENCE WITH THE CORINTHIANS

How many letters did Paul write to the congregation in
Corinth? We might naturally suppose that we could answer this
question merely by referring to the list of contents in the New
Testament itself. This tells us that there were two letters to
the Corinthians. But these letters themselves show us that Paul
wrote to Corinth at least four times. In 1 Cor. 5: 9 he refers
to a previous letter he had sent which had been misunderstood
by its recipients. It seems to have contained a warning against
close contact with pagans. Also, in 2 Cor. 2: 4, he speaks of
another letter which, he says, 'came out of great distress and
anxiety' and over which he had shed 'many tears'. The context shows that it was written to deal with some incident in
which his own authority had been defied. The description of
this letter fits neither the one referred to in 1 Cor. 5: 9 nor
1 Corinthians itself. Certainly Paul had a number of difficult
problems to settle when he wrote 1 Corinthians, but the
general tone is not one of extreme sorrow or anxiety. The
letter of 2 Cor. 2: 4 must therefore have been another letter.
This gives us a total of four: the 'previous letter', 1 Corinthians, the 'painful letter', and 2 Corinthians. There is a
further complication, however. The study of our present
1 Corinthians and 2 Corinthians has suggested to some scholars
that each of these is not one single continuous letter but a
collection of several different letters put together. This theory
requires careful consideration and discussion.

We begin with 1 Corinthians. There are two reasons for
doubting whether this is a single continuous letter. First, it is
said that it contains contradictory opinions on the problem of
idol meat. The Corinthians had asked Paul if it was allowable
for a Christian to eat the meat from an animal which had been

sacrificed to a pagan god. In chapter 8, and also in chapter 10, verses 23–33, he replied that to do so, and even to take part in a feast in a heathen temple, is perfectly legitimate in itself. It is wrong only if it is likely to lead astray one's less enlightened fellow-Christians. But in chapter 10, verses 1–22, he takes a much stricter view. Such practices are idolatry, and anyone who takes part in them is in danger of putting himself in the power of demons. It is argued that he is hardly likely to have contradicted himself so obviously within the space of a few paragraphs and in a single letter. We must therefore suppose that we have here parts of two different letters, later put together by an editor of the Pauline correspondence because they deal with the same topic. The second reason for questioning the unity of 1 Corinthians is that there appears to be no logical connexion between chapter 8 and chapter 9. Chapter 8 is concerned with the problem of idol meat. At the beginning of chapter 9, with no warning at all that he is introducing a fresh topic, Paul plunges straight into a defence of his own conduct as an apostle, a theme which has nothing whatsoever to do with the previous paragraphs. Again, it is argued that chapter 9 must be part of a separate letter, perhaps the one which contained chapter 10, verses 1–22.

These arguments have not been accepted by the majority of scholars, and alternative solutions of the difficulties have been proposed. In the case of the problem of idol meat, it may be that in chapter 8 Paul is for the moment content to argue with his correspondents on their own terms. They may perhaps be right in principle about the harmlessness of taking part in a pagan sacrificial feast, since the pagan god does not really exist. Nevertheless, in practice their action may have a harmful effect on their fellow-Christians. When he comes to write chapter 10 he realizes that they could be wrong in principle as well. The idols represent demons who can be dangerous to their spiritual welfare. The second reason for suspecting the unity of the letter was the apparent lack of connexion between chapter 8 and chapter 9. But it is not true that there is no

4

connexion at all. At the end of chapter 8 Paul has maintained that one should not insist upon one's own individual
rights if to do so is going to hinder other people from living a
Christian life. In chapter 9 he illustrates this principle by
pointing to his own practice. He has refused to claim his
own rights as an apostle (see pp. 66–70). There is therefore no
compelling reason to suppose that 1 Corinthians is a com-
pilation of two or more separate letters rather than a single
continuous one.

The evidence against the unity of 2 Corinthians is somewhat
stronger. In the first place there is no connexion between the
first paragraph of chapter 9 and the opening of chapter 10.
Paul concludes chapter 9 by encouraging the Corinthians to
give generously to the collection he is making for the benefit
of the church in Jerusalem. His tone is entirely friendly.
Chapter 10 opens abruptly and obscurely with a vehement
outburst of self-justification which has nothing to do with the
collection and which at moments suggests that the writer's
attitude to his correspondents is almost hostile. It is this complete change of tone which is more significant than the change
of subject-matter. This brings us to the second reason for
suspecting the unity of the letter. Throughout chapters 10–13
Paul's attitude to his readers is totally different from the attitude he displays in the first nine chapters. The first section of
the letter is friendly and conciliatory; the writer expresses the
utmost confidence in the people he is writing to. But the last
four chapters are vehement and aggressive, and conclude with
the threat of punishment. The difference in tone is striking.
It can be fully appreciated only by a careful reading of the
whole letter. Such a complete alteration of the writer's
attitude is barely credible if it is thought to have taken place
in the course of writing one single letter, especially as no
explanation is given. The lack of logical connexion between
the end of chapter 9 and the beginning of chapter 10 might
possibly be accounted for by supposing that there had been
some slight interruption while the letter was being dictated,

so that a new topic was introduced too abruptly when Paul resumed his dictation. But the change of tone is a more substantial difficulty. It looks as though the only credible explanation would be to say that we have two distinct letters, written at different times in response to different situations.

Attempts have nevertheless been made to explain the difference between the first and the second section of the letter while maintaining its unity. It has been suggested that the change of tone is not, after all, so marked and absolute. The first nine chapters contain hints of reprimand (6: 12–13; 7: 2–3) as well as expressions of affection, and the last four chapters contain affectionate remarks (11: 11; 12: 15) as well as rebukes and warnings. This is true enough. But it hardly seems sufficient to counterbalance the general impression produced by the two sections of the letter as a whole. Another argument is that when Paul appears friendly and optimistic in his attitude towards his converts (chapters 1–9) he is concerned only with their co-operative behaviour in respect of one particular incident which had challenged his authority. In chapters 10–13 he is dealing with a more general opposition on their part which reveals itself in their respect for other missionaries who have set themselves up as his opponents. But if this is so we should not expect to find him saying in 7: 16, 'How happy I am now to have complete confidence in you!' This is an expression of general approval, and cannot be confined to their conduct in one matter only. A more plausible suggestion is that after he had dictated the first nine chapters of the letter he received fresh news from Corinth of a disturbing nature which caused him to change his tone and to write the four concluding chapters. But in that case why did he not revise the first part of the letter, which is friendly in its attitude? The answer to this question is perhaps that it would not have been very easy to do so without rewriting the whole thing. Probably there had been very little space left between the lines of writing or at the margin of the sheets of papyrus where alterations could be made. To rewrite whole sheets at a time would have been a slow process. If the situation in Corinth was urgent, Paul would not want to take time to do this. The letter would be taken to Corinth by one of his personal assistants who could be instructed to explain verbally if any change in the first section of the letter seemed to be desirable.

It is just possible, therefore, to explain the alteration of tone in chapters 10–13 without resorting to the theory that we have two separate letters which were only later put together to form our present 2 Corinthians. Nevertheless, the evidence in favour of the theory is considerable, and its implications need further discussion. If chapters 10–13 are part of some other letter, can we identify it in any way? If 2 Corinthians is a combination of two letters, might it not be a combination of more than two? And how and why did the various letters of which it is composed come to be put together?

Some scholars have identified chapters 10–13 with the 'painful letter' which is mentioned in 2 Cor. 2: 4. The chief reason for doing so is simply that these chapters fit the description of the letter. It was one which had caused Paul some distress of mind to write and which had presumably contained a severe reprimand to the congregation, since it is said to have reduced them to penitence. There is one objection to this identification, however. Nowhere in chapters 10–13 do we find any mention at all of the particular incident which had caused the 'painful letter' to be written. Another suggestion is that these chapters belong to a letter written later than chapters 1–9. This would fit in with various references to Titus which we find in chapters 8 and 12. In 8: 17–18 Titus is about to visit Corinth with an anonymous companion. In 12: 17–18 there is an allusion to a visit which Titus, again with an unnamed companion, has already paid to the city. It looks very much as though it is the same visit which is alluded to in both instances, and in that case chapter 12 was obviously written later than chapter 8. (On the other hand, if we maintain that 2 Corinthians is a unity, it is just possible to suppose that 12: 17–18 refers to a visit paid earlier than the one mentioned in chapter 8 and not to the same one.) Both these suggestions for identifying the hypothetical letter contained in chapters 10–13 have something to be said for them, but neither is conclusive, and the problem remains obscure.

We have so far spoken of chapters 1–9 as though they constituted one single letter. But if we are willing to divide our present 2 Corinthians into two separate letters we must admit the possibility that it may contain more than two. It has been suggested that 6: 14 — 7: 1 is a further separate fragment, since it fails to fit the context in which it now appears. Some scholars would identify it with the 'previous letter' mentioned in 1 Cor. 5: 9. The contents of 6: 14— 7: 1— the prohibition of marriage with unbelievers and the warning against having anything to do with 'the idols of the heathen' —fit in with what we can deduce about this earlier letter from Paul's own reference to it. Part of yet another letter has been detected in the long description of the work of the apostles (2: 14 — 6: 10) which interrupts a series of personal remarks with a digression of some four chapters. If these two suggestions are convincing, we should then be bound to maintain that 2 Corinthians is a collection of at least four separate letters. But at this stage it seems necessary to point out that the kind of argument employed must be used with some caution. Taken to extremes, it would mean that we were ready to detect the existence of a fragment of a separate letter every time we found ourselves momentarily unable to follow Paul's train of thought. But it may be we ourselves who are at fault, in failing to understand the connexion between one paragraph and the next. Or possibly Paul was not always as logical in his train of thought as we expect him to be. In any case, a letter does not necessarily possess the logical coherence which we demand of a philosophical treatise. When we are writing letters ourselves, however serious our intention and our subject-matter, we tend to pass without explanation from one topic to another, expecting our correspondents to understand the link between them or simply to understand that there is no link. Furthermore, the process of dictating a letter was a slow one in Paul's day. There were no shorthand typists in the first century A.D. In addition, Paul had many other duties to attend to. The composition of a long letter such as 2 Corinthians, or even the composition of the first nine chapters, would take a good deal of time and would be subject to frequent interruptions. These factors might very well account for the apparent lack of connexion between some of the paragraphs. They would not, however, account for the complete change of tone between chapters 1–9 and chapters 10–13. We may doubt whether 2 Corinthians contains more than two letters, but we still have to reckon seriously with the possibility that it does contain two.

This presents us with a further problem. How did two (or more) letters come to be put together as one single continuous letter? If they were originally recognizable as separate letters, because they had greetings at the beginning and farewells at the end, why should they not have been put into general circulation as such? It would be altogether too much of a coincidence if they had all accidentally lost their beginnings and endings so that they were assumed to be different parts of a single letter. The problem presents itself even if we are considering only the combination of the first nine and the last four chapters. We should have to suppose that damage had been done both to the last sheet of papyrus on the roll containing 1–9 and also to the first sheet on the roll containing 10–13. One cannot say that it is impossible for this to have happened, but opinions vary as to whether or not it is really probable that it did happen. There is the further possibility that the combination of several letters into one was not accidental but deliberate. This could only have happened at a fairly late date, towards the end of the first century, at a time when Paul's letters were of interest as authoritative doctrinal treatises rather than as personal communications addressed to a particular circle of readers and dealing with a specific local situation. An editor of the Pauline correspondence who was more interested in the apostle's teaching than in the history of his personal relationships with the church at Corinth might have published several short letters as a single continuous one with the idea that one long treatise would be more weighty and impressive. This theory suggests a comparatively late date for the publication of 2 Corinthians. There is supporting evidence for it in the fact that 2 Corinthians became generally known much later than 1 Corinthians. The First Letter of Clement to the Corinthians, written in A.D. 96, and the letters of Ignatius of Antioch, written during the reign of Trajan (A.D. 98–117), show that their authors are familiar with 1 Corinthians but have no knowledge of 2 Corinthians. We can therefore suggest one plausible explanation of the composite nature of 2 Corinthians if we do not believe that it originated as a single continuous letter.

All that can be said in conclusion, however, is that the evidence is very evenly divided and that a definite decision about the unity or otherwise of the letter is difficult to reach.

It is therefore impossible to give a precise answer to the question of how many letters Paul wrote to Corinth. There were certainly at least four, but there may have been as many as seven.

THE DATE AND PLACE OF COMPOSITION

We turn now to the problem of the date and place of composition of the Corinthian correspondence and the reasons for it.

In the case of 1 Corinthians the answers are fairly simple. We know that it was written from Ephesus because Paul himself tells us that he is staying there: 'But I shall remain at Ephesus until Whitsuntide, for a great opportunity has opened for effective work, and there is much opposition' (1 Cor. 16: 8–9). He implies that this is not merely a passing visit but a stay of some duration. When did it take place?

We have said that he arrived in Corinth in A.D. 50. He stayed there for about two years (Acts 18: 11, 18), and then went back to Antioch. After spending some time in Antioch he set out again and eventually arrived at Ephesus (Acts 18:23—19:1). His arrival can presumably be dated in the year A.D. 53. He remained in Ephesus for three years (Acts 20: 31), i.e. from 53 to 56. This means that 1 Corinthians was written sometime during the period A.D. 53–56. The verse we have quoted, which indicates that Paul was planning to leave Ephesus after the Whitsuntide of the year in which he was writing, possibly suggests that the letter was composed towards the end of his stay there, i.e. in 55 or 56.

He had two reasons for writing. In the first place, he had received a visit from some members of the Corinthian congregation whom he calls 'Chloe's people' (1 Cor. 1: 11). It is not clear whether Chloe was a Christian herself. Her 'people' would probably be her household slaves or domestic servants. Whoever they were, they had given Paul disquieting news about what was happening in Corinth. They told him that the congregation was disunited (1: 11–12). They may also have told him of the existence of the other problems which he deals with in the first half of the letter, the case of incest (5: 1), the Corinthians' habit of going to law with each other (6: 1–11), and their indulgence in fornication (6: 12–20). Perhaps he was told of the misbehaviour in public worship which he discusses in chapter 11. Secondly, the Corinthians had themselves written a letter to Paul, asking for his guidance on various points of doctrine and conduct. In the second half of 1 Corinthians we have his reply, beginning with the words, 'And now for the matters you wrote about' (7: 1). They included questions about marriage and divorce (chapter 7), the eating of idol meat (chapter 8), the value of different spiritual gifts (chapters 12–14), and belief in the resurrection (chapter 15).

The question of the date and place of composition of 2 Corinthians is more complicated, since we may be dealing with several letters. If it is reasonable to assume that chapters 1–9 are a continuous whole we can say that they were written from somewhere in Macedonia (2: 13; 7: 5–7) during the journey described in Acts 20: 1–2, immediately after Paul's stay of three years in Ephesus. This would mean that the date of composition was sometime in the year A.D. 57. His reason for writing is to express his satisfaction at the way the congregation has finally dealt with the offender—whoever he was— who had apparently defied his authority and so provoked the 'painful letter' referred to in 2: 4. If the whole of 2 Corinthians is a unity, then we must suppose that, almost as soon as the first nine chapters had been written, Paul received disturbing news from Corinth about further opposition to his authority which caused him to dictate the four final chapters. But if chapters 10–13 are to be identified with the 'painful letter', then they were obviously written earlier, probably while the apostle was still in Ephesus. If they are part of a later letter, the only possibility seems to be that after leaving Ephesus Paul remained in Macedonia for some considerable time, so that he wrote two letters from there, i.e. 2 Cor. 1–9 and 2 Cor. 10–13, with an interval between. The reason for writing chapters 10–13 is plain. Missionaries from elsewhere were influencing the Corinthians, contradicting Paul's own teaching, and undermining his authority. If these chapters comprise the 'painful letter', the missionaries will have been directly concerned in the incident in which his authority had been defied. If chapters 1–9 are to be divided up, we can perhaps say that 6: 14 — 7: 1 can be identified with the 'previous letter', and so was written from Ephesus shortly before 1 Corinthians. If the section 2: 14 — 6: 10 is a separate letter there is no way of discovering when and where it was written.

The following chronological scheme of the Corinthian correspondence is offered as a summary of the preceding arguments rather than as an attempt at a precise dating of the letters.

1. The 'previous letter' (possibly 2 Cor. 6: 14 — 7: 1)	Written from Ephesus, A.D. 53–56
2. A letter from Corinth to Paul	A.D. 53–56
3. 1 Corinthians	A.D. 53–56
4. The 'painful letter' (possibly 2 Cor. 10–13)	A.D. 53–56
5. (*a*) 2 Corinthians *or* (*b*) 2 Cor. 1–9 *or* (*c*) 2 Cor. 1–2: 13; 6: 11–13; 7: 2—9: 15	Written from Macedonia, A.D. 57
6. 2 Cor. 10–13 ?	Written from Macedonia, A.D. 57–58 ?
7. 2 Cor. 2: 14 — 6: 10 ?	Impossible to date

Finally, it is worth drawing attention to a fact which we have casually alluded to already. In all probability Paul dictated most of his letters to one of his companions who acted as his secretary, rather than actually putting pen to paper himself. We know that the Letter to the Romans was dictated, because the scribe who wrote it, a man called Tertius, introduces himself at the end, 'I Tertius, who took this letter down, add my Christian greetings' (Rom. 16: 22). We can also deduce that 1 Corinthians was dictated, because in 16: 21 we have the remark, 'This greeting is in my own hand—PAUL'. This shows that the rest of the letter was not in his own handwriting. In the case of 2 Corinthians, however, there is nothing to show whether Paul dictated it (or the letters it contains) or wrote it in person. We may presume that it was dictated, but there is no definite evidence.

✳　✳　✳　✳　✳　✳　✳　✳　✳　✳　✳　✳　✳

THE FIRST LETTER OF PAUL TO
· THE CORINTHIANS

Unity and Order in the Church

PAUL GREETS THE CHURCH AT CORINTH

1 FROM PAUL, apostle of Jesus Christ at God's call and by God's will, together with our colleague Sosthenes,

2 to the congregation of God's people at Corinth, dedicated to him in Christ Jesus, claimed by him as his own, along with all men everywhere who invoke the name of our Lord Jesus Christ—their Lord as well as ours.

3 Grace and peace to you from God our Father and the Lord Jesus Christ.

4 I am always thanking God for you. I thank him for his

5 grace given to you in Christ Jesus. I thank him for all the enrichment that has come to you in Christ. You possess full knowledge and you can give full expression to it,

6 because in you the evidence for the truth of Christ has

7 found confirmation. There is indeed no single gift you lack, while you wait expectantly for our Lord Jesus Christ

8 to reveal himself. He will keep you firm to the end,

9 without reproach on the Day of our Lord Jesus. It is God himself who called you to share in the life of his Son Jesus Christ our Lord; and God keeps faith.

✻ Paul greets his correspondents and expresses his gratitude for what God has done for them. Ordinary letters of the same period sometimes began with a similar greeting and thanksgiving: 'Dromon to Zenon greeting. I give thanks to all the

14

gods if you are in good health yourself and everything else has been satisfactory.' But the beginning of the present letter is not merely conventional. In about half a dozen sentences Paul mentions several of the major beliefs of Christianity: the idea of the Christian community as God's chosen people, the worship of Christ as Lord, and the expectation of the future return of Christ in glory.

1. Paul does not always introduce himself as an *apostle of Jesus Christ at God's call and by God's will*: 1 Thessalonians, for example, begins simply, 'From Paul, Silvanus, and Timothy to the congregation of Thessalonians....' It will appear later that in his correspondence with Corinth he is compelled to defend himself against people he calls false apostles, who have been influencing the Corinthians and undermining his own authority. It is therefore necessary for him to emphasize at the outset that his authority as an apostle comes from God himself. The word 'apostle' is a Christian technical term, and means 'one who is sent', 'envoy', 'missionary'. It is, however, more restricted in usage than our word 'missionary' suggests. It is applied only to those who had witnessed an appearance of Jesus after his resurrection and had received a divine commission to preach about him. See Acts 26: 12–18 for an account of Paul's own experience.

Sosthenes has sometimes been identified with the man of the same name who is mentioned in Acts 18: 17 as an official of the Jewish synagogue in Corinth. But there is no evidence at all that this man was ever converted to Christianity.

2. In the Old Testament the Israelites are regarded as the nation especially chosen by God to carry out his plans in the world at large. In the New Testament we find that this privilege has been taken away from the Jews as a race and has been transferred to the followers of Jesus Christ. They can therefore be referred to as *the congregation of God's people... dedicated to him in Christ Jesus*. The Greek word *ekklesia* ('church', 'congregation') used in the first of these phrases is found in the Septuagint. This is the Greek version of the Old

Testament used by the Greek-speaking Jews and Christians of Paul's day. The word is used in the translation of the Hebrew phrase which means 'the congregation of the Lord', i.e. the nation of Israel in its capacity as God's chosen people. The fact that this term is now applicable to the Christian community is underlined by the phrase *claimed by him as his own*. More literally translated it runs 'called to be holy'. One of the meanings of the word 'holy' is 'set apart for the service of God'. The Israelites were a 'holy nation' in this sense (Exod. 19: 6), and the Christian community, likewise, is separated from the rest of the world and placed completely at God's disposal. Christians are also described in this verse as those *who invoke the name of our Lord Jesus Christ*. In the Old Testament to 'invoke the name' of God means to worship him. The use of the expression here suggests that the followers of Jesus had begun to worship him as divine (see pp. 62–3).

4–7. *grace* is God's overwhelming kindness towards us—a kindness which we have done nothing whatsoever to deserve. It is shown to us by Jesus Christ. In the life of the individual Christian the result of God's kindness is the possession of such gifts as *full knowledge* of the meaning of the Christian faith and the ability to pass on this understanding to others.

5. The phrase *in Christ* means 'as a member of the Church'. Paul later refers to the Church as the Body of Christ. It is in some way a part of Christ's own personality (see 12: 12–31). All the divine powers and all the qualities of character which belong to Jesus Christ himself are passed on to the members of the Christian community, so that in a real sense they *share in the life* of the Son of God (verse 9).

7–8. The early Christians believed that Jesus would very shortly return to earth and *reveal himself* in his true state of supernatural glory. This event is spoken of as *the Day of our Lord Jesus*. The expression calls to mind the idea of the Day of the Lord in the Old Testament. This was a time when God would appear in glory and majesty to judge and punish the wicked (Isa. 2: 10–21). It was the day when his kingly rule would be re-established. All forms of evil would be destroyed, and it would be the beginning of the glorious future to which everyone looked forward. In the world of nature this meant the defeat of the forces of decay and death, and a miraculous increase of the fertility of the ground. On the political level it was thought to mean the defeat of Israel's enemies and the beginning of a period of national security and prosperity. The prophets, however, warned the Israelites that it would be a day of 'darkness' (Amos 5: 18) to Israel too, because of her failure to obey God's will. Later Jews thought that it would be possible to abolish evil only if the present world were completely destroyed. From their point of view the Day of the Lord becomes the final judgement at the end of history. The Christian writers of the New Testament also think of the Day of the Lord as the end of the world. But in Christian thought Christ has taken over the functions which were previously ascribed to God. It is Christ who is to appear in glory and to act as judge. ✻

DISUNITY IN THE CONGREGATION

I appeal to you, my brothers, in the name of our Lord 10 Jesus Christ: agree among yourselves, and avoid divisions; be firmly joined in unity of mind and thought. I have 11 been told, my brothers, by Chloe's people that there are quarrels among you. What I mean is this: each of you 12 is saying, 'I am Paul's man', or 'I am for Apollos'; 'I follow Cephas', or 'I am Christ's.' Surely Christ has not 13 been divided among you! Was it Paul who was cruci-fied for you? Was it in the name of Paul that you were baptized? Thank God, I never baptized one of you— 14 except Crispus and Gaius. So no one can say you were 15 baptized in my name.—Yes, I did baptize the household 16 of Stephanas; I cannot think of anyone else. Christ did not 17 send me to baptize, but to proclaim the Gospel; and to do it without relying on the language of worldly wisdom, so that the fact of Christ on his cross might have its full weight.

✻ The first problem which faces Paul is that the congregation at Corinth has split into groups. Each group claimed to be led by a different apostle. Paul tactfully takes his own supporters as the target of his criticism, and points out the obvious fact that it was not he who died on their behalf. Their fervent allegiance to an individual apostle contradicts their common loyalty to Christ who was crucified for them.

12. The members of one group claimed '*I am Paul's man*'. They were probably his original converts. Perhaps they saw that his authority was being undermined and had for this reason formed themselves into a definite party to support him. Others asserted '*I am for Apollos*'. The story of Apollos is told in Acts 18: 24–8. He was an eloquent speaker, skilled in the interpretation of Scripture. He may have gained supporters in Corinth, unintentionally, because some members of the congregation preferred his style of preaching to that of Paul. These two Church leaders had both spent some time in Corinth, but there is no evidence that the apostle next mentioned, *Cephas* (i.e. Peter), had ever visited the church there. His followers were possibly Jewish Christians who had emigrated from Palestine. The last group consists of those who say '*I am Christ's*'. This presents a difficulty: Paul appears to blame them just as much as he does those who declare their support for Cephas, Apollos or himself; yet in the following verses he insists that it is to Christ alone that Christians owe their allegiance. The answer may be that in some way this group had turned Christ himself into a kind of party-leader on the same level as, and in opposition to, Peter and Paul, and so reduced Christ's supreme authority over the whole congregation. Perhaps the distinguishing feature of the Christ-party was that they claimed to be independent of Paul's authority on the grounds that they received a special inward and spiritual

18

guidance from Christ himself which was not given to the rest of the church.

13. The Corinthians give the impression that they have shared out Paul, Apollos, Peter, and even Christ himself, and have distributed them among the members of the congregation so that each belongs to one group only. In the case of Christ this is an obvious absurdity. Christ belongs to the whole congregation, since they all belong to him as a result of their baptism.

13-17. The reason why Paul insists that his converts were not baptized in his *name* is that the 'name' was a sign of ownership. As we see from Acts (2: 38; 10: 48), converts were baptized in the name of Jesus Christ, which meant that Christ owned them as a master owned slaves. Paul may also be correcting a misunderstanding of baptism which had led his readers to suppose that the baptizer gained some special authority over the person he baptized.

14. *Crispus* was a former synagogue official who had become a Christian (Acts 18: 8). *Gaius* was Paul's host in Corinth (Rom. 16: 23).

16. *Stephanas* is mentioned again at the end of the letter (16: 15-18).

17. The reference to *worldly wisdom* points forward to the argument of the next section. ✳

DIVINE WISDOM AND HUMAN WISDOM

This doctrine of the cross is sheer folly to those on their 18 way to ruin, but to us who are on the way to salvation it is the power of God. Scripture says, 'I will destroy the 19 wisdom of the wise, and bring to nothing the cleverness of the clever.' Where is your wise man now, your man 20 of learning, or your subtle debater—limited, all of them, to this passing age? God has made the wisdom of this world look foolish. As God in his wisdom ordained, 21

the world failed to find him by its wisdom, and he chose
to save those who have faith by the folly of the Gospel.
22,23 Jews call for miracles, Greeks look for wisdom; but we
proclaim Christ—yes, Christ nailed to the cross; and though
this is a stumbling-block to Jews and folly to Greeks,
24 yet to those who have heard his call, Jews and Greeks
alike, he is the power of God and the wisdom of God.

25 Divine folly is wiser than the wisdom of man, and
26 divine weakness stronger than man's strength. My
brothers, think what sort of people you are, whom God
has called. Few of you are men of wisdom, by any
27 human standard; few are powerful or highly born. Yet,
to shame the wise, God has chosen what the world counts
folly, and to shame what is strong, God has chosen what
28 the world counts weakness. He has chosen things low
and contemptible, mere nothings, to overthrow the
29 existing order. And so there is no place for human pride
30 in the presence of God. You are in Christ Jesus by God's
act, for God has made him our wisdom; he is our
righteousness; in him we are consecrated and set free.
31 And so (in the words of Scripture), 'If a man is proud,
let him be proud of the Lord.'

✶ Paul's insistence that his main task is to 'proclaim the Gospel'
(verse 17) leads him to consider the basic theme of his preaching, 'the fact of Christ on his cross'. As a result of the death of
Christ, the personal relationship of men and women with God
is put right and becomes what God originally intended it to
be (verse 30). By means of the crucifixion, God is actively and
effectively carrying out his plan for the ultimate good of the
human race. This event can therefore be said to demonstrate
both God's *power* and God's *wisdom*. Further, since Jesus
was no passive victim but willingly co-operated in the

achievement of God's purpose, Paul can speak of Christ as being himself *the power of God and the wisdom of God* (verse 24). But this divine wisdom is the complete opposite of human wisdom: to the world at large, Jews and non-Jews alike, the Christian message is sheer stupidity (verses 18, 22–3). Nevertheless, in three ways God is showing up the *wisdom* of the *world* as being itself foolish. First, the philosophers and men of learning, for all their cleverness, were not able by means of their own wisdom to discover what God is like (verse 21). Secondly, the preaching of the Gospel is having a real effect (verses 18, 21, 24). Thirdly, God has chosen people to put his plans into action who by human standards are powerless and insignificant (verses 26–8). All this shows that pride in purely human achievements is entirely out of place; we can be proud only of what God himself has done for us (verses 29–31).

19. The quotation is from the Greek version of Isa. 29: 14. The English versions follow the Hebrew, which runs: 'and the wisdom of their wise men shall perish, and the understanding of their prudent men shall be hid'.

23. The fact that Jesus had been crucified would hinder the majority of Jews from accepting him as Messiah because they expected the Messiah to drive the Romans from Palestine, whereas Jesus had been executed by them. Moreover, according to the Law of Moses (Deut. 21: 23) a crucified person was considered to be under God's curse (cf. Gal. 3: 13). Cultured pagans, with the example of Socrates in mind, might well admire Jesus as a wise and good teacher unjustly put to death. But the idea that his death was itself part of a divine plan for the welfare of mankind would be sheer stupidity to such people as these.

30. The word *righteousness* is not used here in the sense of moral goodness of character. Behind it there lies the picture of the defendant in the law-court who obtains a verdict of 'righteous', i.e. 'not guilty'. Christ saves the Christian from being found guilty in God's court of law at the last judgement. If we translate the legal idea into the more important terms of

personal relationships, it means that Christ gains for us God's forgiveness, and so repairs the broken relationship which has previously existed between ourselves and God. Notice, however, that all the way through these two paragraphs Christ's actions are God's actions as well. It is God himself who makes the first move in the process of reconciliation. When our relationship with God is put right in this way we are *consecrated* to his service. The meaning here is the same as that of the phrases in verse 2: 'dedicated to him in Christ Jesus', and 'claimed by him as his own'. We are also *set free*. Literally, Christ is our 'redemption'. This word originally referred to the deliverance of prisoners or the liberation of slaves upon payment of a ransom or the purchase price. In the Old Testament the verb 'redeem' is used metaphorically of God's act of deliverance when he freed the Hebrews from slavery in Egypt. This was a political liberation. In the New Testament the act of deliverance, the 'redemption', has become a spiritual one. As a result of what Christ has done for us we are liberated from the tyrannical power of evil tendencies which previously dominated us as a master dominates slaves.

31. This is a précis of Jer. 9: 23–4. ✳

PAUL'S FIRST VISIT TO CORINTH

2 As for me, brothers, when I came to you, I declared the attested truth of God without display of fine words or
2 wisdom. I resolved that while I was with you I would think of nothing but Jesus Christ—Christ nailed to the
3 cross. I came before you weak, as I was then, nervous
4 and shaking with fear. The word I spoke, the gospel I proclaimed, did not sway you with subtle arguments; it
5 carried conviction by spiritual power, so that your faith might be built not upon human wisdom but upon the power of God.

✻ Paul himself has shown the Corinthians that God is infinitely more powerful than human beings, however wise or eloquent they might be by human standards. When he first preached to them he did not use ingenious philosophical arguments or fine and eloquent phrases, but told them simply about the crucifixion of Jesus. Nevertheless, they were convinced of the truth of what he said. But this was because he was inspired by God, not because of his own *human wisdom*.

3. The impression Paul made was not due to his own personal qualities. When he says that he was *weak*, he may be referring to a physical ailment of some kind which hindered his work from time to time, and which he describes in 2 Cor. 12: 7 as 'a sharp pain in my body'. His personal appearance was probably unimpressive, if we are to believe the description of him given by a Christian writer of the late second century in a book entitled the *Acts of Paul*: 'a man little of stature, thin-haired upon the head, crooked in the legs, of good state of body, with eyebrows joining, and nose somewhat hooked'. ✻

CHRISTIAN WISDOM

And yet I do speak words of wisdom to those who are 6 ripe for it, not a wisdom belonging to this passing age, nor to any of its governing powers, which are declining to their end; I speak God's hidden wisdom, his secret pur- 7 pose framed from the very beginning to bring us to our full glory. The powers that rule the world have never 8 known it; if they had, they would not have crucified the Lord of glory. But, in the words of Scripture, 'Things 9 beyond our seeing, things beyond our hearing, things beyond our imagining, all prepared by God for those who love him', these it is that God has revealed to us through 10 the Spirit.

For the Spirit explores everything, even the depths of
11 God's own nature. Among men, who knows what a
man is but the man's own spirit within him? In the same
12 way, only the Spirit of God knows what God is. This is
the Spirit that we have received from God, and not the
spirit of the world, so that we may know all that God of
13 his own grace gives us; and, because we are interpreting
spiritual truths to those who have the Spirit, we speak
of these gifts of God in words found for us not by our
14 human wisdom but by the Spirit. A man who is unspiritual refuses what belongs to the Spirit of God; it is
folly to him; he cannot grasp it, because it needs to be
15 judged in the light of the Spirit. A man gifted with the
Spirit can judge the worth of everything, but is not
16 himself subject to judgement by his fellow-men. For (in
the words of Scripture) 'who knows the mind of the
Lord? Who can advise him?' We, however, possess the
mind of Christ.

✫ Despite all that has been said about the limitations of human wisdom, we are not to suppose that Christians must altogether abandon the idea of acquiring *wisdom* of any sort. There is a Christian form of wisdom in which Paul instructs those who have already learned the basic principles of Christianity. It has two characteristics. First, it is a knowledge of truths which God himself has revealed to the apostles and their converts, not something they have discovered or invented themselves. Secondly, it can be understood only by those who are inspired by God to do so; to anyone who lacks this divine guidance, Christian wisdom is sheer nonsense.

6–8. There are two ideas which need explanation before we can understand these verses as a whole. First Paul speaks of *this passing age*. He is alluding to the belief of the Jews that

the whole of time was divided into two periods: This Age and
The Age to Come. This Age, i.e. the time in which they
themselves were living, was a time of universal wickedness and
hostility towards God. The Age to Come would be the time
when God himself would take action to put things right and
to put an end to all the evil in the world. It was sometimes
thought that he would do this by destroying the present world
entirely and creating a new one. For Christians, The Age to
Come has already in some sense begun (which is why Paul can
speak of This Age as *passing*). By sending Jesus, God has
begun to deal with the problem of evil. He offers men forgiveness, and the possibility of a new kind of existence in
which they are free from the domination of sin (cf. 1: 30).
Nevertheless, although This Age is therefore drawing to its
close, it has not yet completely come to an end. The work of
Christ in getting rid of evil is still not finished. So for the
Christian the two ages overlap. The end-period of This Age
coincides with the beginning of The Age to Come.

Secondly, this Age has its own *governing powers, powers
that rule the world*. What is meant by these phrases? It is
possible that Paul is simply referring to the ordinary human
political authorities of his day, i.e. the Roman Emperor
and the various subordinate princes and magistrates who
administered the provinces of the Empire on his behalf. He
says that these powers *crucified the Lord of glory*, and it was
certainly the Roman governor of Judaea, representing the
Emperor Tiberius, who had given the order for the execution of Jesus of Nazareth. But there may be a further
idea present as well. The Jews believed that This Age was
under the control of evil supernatural powers, non-human
spiritual beings who were disobedient to God. There is an
allusion to this belief in 1 John 5: 19, 'the whole godless world
lies in the power of the evil one'. It is a view which Paul himself shared. Elsewhere in his correspondence he describes the
death of Christ as a battle fought on God's behalf against these
supernatural powers who were thought to dominate the world

(Col. 2: 15). It is very probable that he supposed Pontius Pilate to be acting as their human instrument when he brought about the crucifixion. There is therefore a double reference here, both to the supernatural powers and to human authorities.

Christian wisdom is *not a wisdom belonging to this passing age*. It is completely incomprehensible to those who know nothing about Christ and so live their lives entirely within the boundaries of This Age, without any experience of The Age to Come. People who live in This Age are hostile towards God, and this state of mind results in moral and intellectual blindness: 'all their thinking has ended in futility, and their misguided minds are plunged in darkness' (Rom. 1: 21). The philosophical systems they invent are astray from the truth, and the real truth is something they are incapable of understanding. Christian wisdom is therefore absolutely alien to them. Nor do the powers which govern the world understand it. This is proved by the fact that they were responsible for the crucifixion. Christian wisdom is a knowledge of God's *secret purpose*, his plan for the ultimate welfare of mankind. Now the death of Christ was essential if the plan was to be put into effect. If the governing powers had known about it they would not have engineered the crucifixion. They are in a state of opposition to God and would not wish to assist him to achieve his object. Paul does not explain in any detail exactly what this knowledge or wisdom consists of. He defines it simply as the understanding of God's intention *to bring us to our full glory*. The term *glory* refers to the condition of bodily and spiritual splendour in which Christians will exist after they have been raised from the dead. It is a state of being which will be a reproduction and a reflexion of the glory of God himself. In biblical language the 'glory' of God often means the nature and character of God. Therefore, to say that Christians will reflect God's glory means that in the end they will be like him in character. Now we see a perfect image of the nature of God in the character of Jesus. It is the character of Jesus which is eventually to be faithfully and completely reproduced in the characters of his followers. This is a process which begins here and now and is finally completed in the life of the resurrection. Christian wisdom might therefore be described as the knowledge of how this transformation begins to take place in the present and of what its results will be in the future.

9–10. These *words of Scripture* are a very free quotation of Isa. 64: 4 and 65: 17.

10–16. God has *revealed* his *secret purpose* to Paul and his fellow-Christians *through the Spirit*. This paragraph describes *the Spirit* in two different ways. First, God has a spirit just as man has. When Paul speaks of a *man's own spirit* he is thinking of the fact that human beings possess self-consciousness. We can think about ourselves and reflect upon our own motives and feelings and character. Our human spirits have the power of understanding what kind of people we are. In the same way, the Spirit of God understands the nature of God. According to Paul, a man understands himself better than anyone else can understand him: *who knows what a man is but the man's own spirit within him?* Likewise, the Spirit explores *the depths of God's own nature*, and *only the Spirit of God knows what God is*. Secondly, the Spirit is a gift given to man, a divine power inspiring him. This view of the Spirit resembles the Old Testament descriptions of God's Spirit, particularly as it is spoken of by the prophet Isaiah. He says about the ideal future king: 'and the spirit of the Lord shall rest upon him, the spirit of wisdom and understanding, the spirit of counsel and might, the spirit of knowledge and of the fear of the Lord' (Isa. 11: 2).

God's Spirit, therefore, is both his own power of self-consciousness and also the gift of spiritual insight given to man so that he can understand God. We ourselves can pass on our understanding of ourselves to other people so that they know what we are like. By talking to my friends about my aims and opinions and feelings I show what sort of a person I am, so that they understand my character. In the same way, God passes on to us his knowledge of his own nature so that we begin to understand him. We possess his Spirit as a gift he has given us. Now Christ has a complete understanding of the nature of God. Therefore, those to whom God has given his Spirit can be described as those who *possess the mind of Christ*. They are able to judge every situation as God would judge it, and to see things as God sees them. The man who does not possess the Spirit is unable to do this, and cannot understand God. But such a person has no right to pass judgement upon those who do possess the Spirit, since this would be the same thing as passing judgement upon God himself. No human being has the right to do this. In verse 16 Paul quotes from Isa. 40: 13 to show that no one can presume to instruct God or to understand his ways unaided. ✳

THE PROBLEM OF DISUNITY AGAIN

3 For my part, my brothers, I could not speak to you as I should speak to people who have the Spirit. I had to deal with you on the merely natural plane, as infants in Christ.
2 And so I gave you milk to drink, instead of solid food, for which you were not yet ready. Indeed, you are still not
3 ready for it, for you are still on the merely natural plane. Can you not see that while there is jealousy and strife among you, you are living on the purely human level of
4 your lower nature? When one says, 'I am Paul's man', and another, 'I am for Apollos', are you not all too human?

5   After all, what is Apollos? What is Paul? We are simply God's agents in bringing you to the faith. Each of
6 us performed the task which the Lord allotted to him: I planted the seed, and Apollos watered it; but God made

it grow. Thus it is not the gardeners with their planting 7
and watering who count, but God, who makes it grow.
Whether they plant or water, they work as a team, 8
though each will get his own pay for his own labour.
We are God's fellow-workers; and you are God's garden. 9

✻ More needs to be said about the evils of party factions. In
the first place, the ill-feeling which they have generated is
causing the Corinthians to behave in a sub-Christian way.
Secondly, their existence means that the importance of the
apostles has been greatly exaggerated. In reality it is God himself who has brought into being the Christian community in
Corinth. The apostles have merely prepared the ground for
his work.

1–4. The contrast Paul has just drawn between a person
'gifted with the Spirit' and one who is 'unspiritual' (2: 14–15)
brings him back to the actual state of affairs in Corinth. It is
clear that he believes his converts to have received the gift of
the Spirit (3: 16; 6: 11, 19; 12: 13). Nevertheless it is painfully
obvious that they are not behaving like *people who have the
Spirit*. They lack spiritual understanding, so that he has been
able to instruct them only in the more elementary aspects of
the Christian faith, feeding them, like children, with *milk*
rather than *solid food*. Worse still, their party factions have
given rise to *jealousy and strife*. As Paul writes in another letter,
the gift of the Spirit should produce in the Christian such
qualities as love, peace, patience, kindness and gentleness
(Gal. 5: 22). If these qualities are lacking in the lives of the
Corinthians it gives the impression that they do not possess
the Spirit at all. They are still *living on the purely human level* of
their *lower nature* (verse 3). More literally translated, this verse
would run: 'you are fleshly and you behave in accordance
with human standards'. The word 'fleshly', paraphrased in
the N.E.B. by terms such as *lower nature* and *on the merely
natural plane*, does not necessarily describe people who indulge
in physical vices—'sins of the flesh' in the popular sense of the

phrase. Nor does the translators' term *lower nature* mean that the human personality is divided up into a 'higher' part consisting of the mind and spirit and a 'lower' part consisting of the physical impulses. For Paul, 'the flesh' is often a symbolic expression standing for mankind and indicating that man is totally different from God. God is spirit; he is all powerful and immortal. Man is flesh; in himself he is weak and destined to die. There is also a further difference between God and man. God is holy and man is sinful. Human beings have deliberately disobeyed God and separated themselves from him. The term 'flesh' stands for this characteristic of human life as well. Therefore, those who are 'fleshly' are those who have chosen to turn their back on God and so to live in a state of separation from him. This means that they become worldly minded and materialistic. They may perhaps indulge in physical sins such as fornication and drunkenness. But their 'fleshly' condition is a condition of their whole personality. It affects their mind and will, their spirit and their emotions, and leads to such 'non-physical' sins as idolatry and sorcery, selfish ambitions and party intrigues and the like (Gal. 5: 20). And a man's *lower nature* is his whole personality, his whole self, when he is thinking and behaving in a 'fleshly' way. Furthermore, this is the 'natural' way for men to think and behave unless they possess the gift of the Spirit. The Corinthians, by reason of their jealousy and party strife, have been slipping back into 'natural' forms of behaviour and denying by implication their possession of the Spirit. ✶

WARNING OF JUDGEMENT

10 Or again, you are God's building. I am like a skilled master-builder who by God's grace laid the foundation, and someone else is putting up the building. Let each
11 take care how he builds. There can be no other foundation beyond that which is already laid; I mean Jesus Christ
12 himself. If anyone builds on that foundation with gold,

silver, and fine stone, or with wood, hay, and straw, the 13
work that each man does will at last be brought to light;
the day of judgement will expose it. For that day dawns
in fire, and the fire will test the worth of each man's work.
If a man's building stands, he will be rewarded; if it 14,15
burns, he will have to bear the loss; and yet he will
escape with his life, as one might from a fire. Surely you 16
know that you are God's temple, where the Spirit of
God dwells. Anyone who destroys God's temple will 17
himself be destroyed by God, because the temple of God
is holy; and that temple you are.

Make no mistake about this: if there is anyone among 18
you who fancies himself wise—wise, I mean, by the
standards of this passing age—he must become a fool to
gain true wisdom. For the wisdom of this world is folly 19
in God's sight. Scripture says, 'He traps the wise in their
own cunning', and again, 'The Lord knows that the 20
arguments of the wise are futile.' So never make mere men 21
a cause for pride. For though everything belongs to you
—Paul, Apollos, and Cephas, the world, life, and death, 22
the present and the future, all of them belong to you—
yet you belong to Christ, and Christ to God.   23

✻ Although Paul has emphasized the unimportance of the
individual apostles he nevertheless seems to think it necessary
to assert his own apostolic authority as the founder of the
Corinthian church. The rest of chapter 3 and the whole of
chapter 4 are concerned with a justification of his own work
and that of his fellow-apostles. He is fighting as it were on
two fronts. On the one hand, he must put a stop to the
divisions within the congregation. These have resulted in the
formation of groups who are attached in a partisan spirit to
Apollos, Cephas and himself. On the other hand, he also has

to deal with a tendency to break away from apostolic control altogether. He begins by warning those who are now teaching and influencing his converts that the worth of what they are doing will eventually be judged. If they attempt to alter the basic principles of belief and practice which he has established they will be condemned for it.

10–13. The various elements in the image of the *building* are as follows. The *building* itself is the Christian community in Corinth. The *foundation* is Paul's original teaching about Christ which, humanly speaking, caused the community to come into being. The other builders are the present teachers and leaders of the congregation. Those who use *gold, silver, and fine stone* as their building materials are those whose work will be really profitable. Those who build with *hay, and straw* are those who are accomplishing nothing of lasting value.

13. All this will be made clear on *the day of judgement*, i.e. the 'Day of our Lord Jesus' (1: 8). The idea that the day of judgement would be like a fire is a common one. We find it in the Old Testament in Malachi: 'For, behold, the day cometh, it burneth as a furnace' (Mal. 4: 1). In the New Testament it occurs in 2 Peter: 'that day will set the heavens ablaze until they fall apart, and will melt the elements in flames' (2 Pet. 3: 12).

14–15. The fire metaphor is easily applied to the image of the building. The fire will destroy the walls built of shoddy material. In other words, the moment of judgement will reveal the worthlessness of some of the church work which is now being done. Those responsible for it will suffer in some way, though Paul does not explain what their punishment will be. He does insist, however, that they will not be finally condemned to personal destruction, along with those who are evil without hope of amendment; *he will escape with his life, as one might from a fire.*

16–17. We now have a much sterner warning against those who would intentionally destroy the Christian life of the community. Probably Paul has in mind the people who are encouraging the party factions. In order to show how serious their offence is, he points out that intentional damage to the life of the Church is the same thing as desecrating a temple. In the pagan world the gods were thought to live in their temples and to avenge themselves upon those who failed to show a proper reverence for sacred places. From the Christian point of view, the Church, i.e. the Christian community, is the real *temple* of the true God. Christians are in direct contact with God because they are inspired by the Spirit of God, and so the Church is the place where God is to be found. It is sacred, and those who corrupt it will be punished by God himself.

18–23. It looks as though the people who *make mere men a cause for pride*, i.e. those who are promoting the divisions in the congregation, are also those who pride themselves on their *wisdom*. Paul quotes Scripture (Job 5: 13; Ps. 94: 11) to prove that God regards this sort of wisdom as foolish. It is a mistaken attitude to exaggerate the importance of one or another of the apostles and set him up on a pedestal. The apostles are the servants of the Church and in that sense it is they who *belong* to the Corinthians, not the Corinthians to them as followers and servants of individual party-leaders. But it is not only the apostles who might be said to exist for the benefit of the Christian community. Every possible experience in life, and even the experience of death itself, *belongs* to Christians, in the sense that in the end it will turn out to be for their good. Every experience which a Christian may undergo is therefore his servant, but he himself is a servant to Christ, and Christ is the servant of God. ✳

THE DAILY LIFE OF AN APOSTLE

We must be regarded as Christ's underlings and as **4** stewards of the secrets of God. Well then, stewards are 2 expected to show themselves trustworthy. For my part, 3 if I am called to account by you or by any human court

of judgement, it does not matter to me in the least. Why,
4 I do not even pass judgement on myself, for I have nothing on my conscience; but that does not mean I stand
5 acquitted. My judge is the Lord. So pass no premature
judgement; wait until the Lord comes. For he will bring
to light what darkness hides, and disclose men's inward
motives; then will be the time for each to receive from
God such praise as he deserves.

6 Into this general picture, my friends, I have brought
Apollos and myself on your account, so that you may
take our case as an example, and learn to 'keep within the
rules', as they say, and may not be inflated with pride as
7 you patronize one and flout the other. Who makes you,
my friend, so important? What do you possess that was
not given you? If then you really received it all as a gift,
why take the credit to yourself?

8 All of you, no doubt, have everything you could
desire. You have come into your fortune already. You
have come into your kingdom—and left us out. How I
wish you had indeed won your kingdom; then you
9 might share it with us! For it seems to me God has made
us apostles the most abject of mankind. We are like men
condemned to death in the arena, a spectacle to the whole
10 universe—angels as well as men. We are fools for Christ's
sake, while you are such sensible Christians. We are
weak; you are so powerful. We are in disgrace; you are
11 honoured. To this day we go hungry and thirsty and in
rags; we are roughly handled; we wander from place to
12 place; we wear ourselves out working with our own
hands. They curse us, and we bless; they persecute us,
13 and we submit to it; they slander us, and we humbly

make our appeal. We are treated as the scum of the earth, the dregs of humanity, to this very day.

✱ The defence of the apostles and their work is continued. Paul insists that his converts have no right to pass judgement on what he himself has done. He also points to the hardships which the apostles endure, and to their despised and insignificant position in human society, and so condemns the arrogance and self-satisfaction displayed by the Corinthians.

1. This verse links the present section with the preceding one. The apostles are 'mere men' (3: 21), and comparatively unimportant; they are no 'cause for pride'. They are simply Christ's *underlings*. The term *stewards* suggests the same idea, since in the ancient world stewards were frequently slaves. But the use of this term suggests a second line of thought, which is developed in the following verses.

2. A steward was expected to be *trustworthy*. He managed an estate or a household on his master's behalf and possessed a certain amount of authority. He was responsible only to his master, to whom he had to give an account of the way he had carried out his duties. (For an example, see the parable in Luke 16: 1–8). The apostles manage the missionary work of the Church on behalf of Christ, their master, to whom they are responsible for the way in which they have employed the authority he has delegated to them. They also must be trustworthy.

3–5. They are not, however, responsible to any one else for the performance of their duties. It is only Christ, their master, who has the right to call them to account and pass judgement on them.

6–7. Paul draws attention to his own humble estimate of his importance as an individual (3: 5)—an attitude of mind we may suppose *Apollos* to have shared. He does so in order to warn his converts against the *pride* and spiritual arrogance which leads them not only to *flout* an apostle of whom they disapprove but also to *patronize* the one whom they profess to support. The reason for their pride is probably their possession of the various 'spiritual gifts' which are discussed in detail at a later point in the letter (chapters 12 and 14). But this is really no reason at all. Their 'gifts' are precisely that—gifts of God, not their own achievement.

8–13. What is the point of this contrast between the happy state the readers of the letter suppose themselves to have achieved and the hardships endured daily by the apostles? Probably it is meant to show that, since for the apostles the consequences of following Christ are humiliation and suffering, this ought to be in some degree true of the Corinthians, if they are genuinely Christian themselves. It follows that their condition of comfortable security is an illusion, or else that they are not as Christian as they suppose themselves to be. At any rate, they have no right to feel self-satisfied, nor to regard themselves as superior to the apostles.

8. Their notion that they have *come into* their *kingdom* perhaps refers to the belief that Christ's followers would eventually share in his rule over the world. In the present letter this comes to light in 6: 2–3, where we find the idea that the Church will share Christ's function of judgement at the end of the world (see also Rev. 20: 4–6). The Corinthians must have supposed that they already shared Christ's authority. ✻

THE MISSION OF TIMOTHY

14 I am not writing thus to shame you, but to bring you to
15 reason; for you are my dear children. You may have ten thousand tutors in Christ, but you have only one father. For in Christ Jesus you are my offspring, and mine alone,
16 through the preaching of the Gospel. I appeal to you
17 therefore to follow my example. That is the very reason why I have sent Timothy, who is a dear son to me and a most trustworthy Christian; he will remind you of the way of life in Christ which I follow, and which I teach
18 everywhere in all our congregations. There are certain

persons who are filled with self-importance because they
think I am not coming to Corinth. I shall come very soon, 19
if the Lord will; and then I shall take the measure of these
self-important people, not by what they say, but by what
power is in them. The kingdom of God is not a matter 20
of talk, but of power. Choose, then: am I to come to 21
you with a rod in my hand, or in love and a gentle spirit?

✱ 14–15. Paul writes as a *father* who is concerned for the welfare of his *children*. Life as a Christian was so radically different
from one's previous existence that, as the Fourth Gospel puts
it (John 3: 3), to be converted was to be 'born over again'. It
is the *preaching* of the apostles which causes this rebirth to take
place, and so they can be described as the spiritual fathers of
their converts. *In Christ Jesus* means 'as Christians' and 'as
members of the Church'—in Paul's view the two things are
inseparable. Those who are at present influencing the Corinthians in their interpretation of Christianity cannot be described
as their 'fathers': they are merely in the position of *tutors*. The
Greek word *paidagogos*, here translated 'tutor', did not in fact
refer to a teacher, as we might have expected. The *paidagogos*
was a slave whose job it was to accompany a boy of good
family to school and to supervise his behaviour in general.
By using this metaphor Paul is insisting on his own greatly
superior claim to his converts' obedience, since he himself is in
the position of the father of the family.

17. There is some information about *Timothy* in Acts 16:
1–3. His home was in Lystra, and he is described as 'the son
of a Jewish Christian mother and a Greek father'. Since Paul
here speaks of him as his *dear son* it would appear that he had
himself been responsible for his conversion. Timothy then
became Paul's companion and assistant. In other letters his
name is given at the beginning as joint-author (2 Corinthians,
Philippians, Colossians, 1 Thessalonians, 2 Thessalonians).

20. *The kingdom of God* means the rule of God over the

37

world. God is king, but not all his subjects acknowledge his authority and obey him. It was the task of Jesus and his followers to establish God's kingdom by persuading men and women to abandon their rebellious attitude towards him. For this task, mere human *talk* was insufficient. It was necessary to possess *power*, i.e. the power of the Spirit of God, which alone made the apostles' preaching effective (2: 4–5). Paul doubts whether the *self-important people* at Corinth possess this power. ✶

THE CASE OF INCEST

5 I actually hear reports of sexual immorality among you, immorality such as even pagans do not tolerate: the union
2 of a man with his father's wife. And you can still be proud of yourselves! You ought to have gone into mourning; a man who has done such a deed should have
3 been rooted out of your company. For my part, though I am absent in body, I am present in spirit, and my judgement upon the man who did this thing is already
4 given, as if I were indeed present: you all being assembled in the name of our Lord Jesus, and I with you in spirit,
5 with the power of our Lord Jesus over us, this man is to be consigned to Satan for the destruction of the body, so that his spirit may be saved on the Day of the Lord.

6 Your self-satisfaction ill becomes you. Have you never heard the saying, 'A little leaven leavens all the dough'?
7 The old leaven of corruption is working among you. Purge it out, and then you will be bread of a new baking, as it were unleavened Passover bread. For indeed our Passover has begun; the sacrifice is offered—Christ him-
8 self. So we who observe the festival must not use the old leaven, the leaven of corruption and wickedness, but only the unleavened bread which is sincerity and truth.

In my letter I wrote that you must have nothing to do 9
with loose livers. I was not, of course, referring to pagans 10
who lead loose lives or are grabbers and swindlers or
idolaters. To avoid them you would have to get right out
of the world. I now write that you must have nothing 11
to do with any so-called Christian who leads a loose life,
or is grasping, or idolatrous, a slanderer, a drunkard, or a
swindler. You should not even eat with any such person.
What business of mine is it to judge outsiders? God is 12,13
their judge. You are judges within the fellowship. Root
out the evil-doer from your community.

* Disunity was not the only problem to be dealt with. A
particularly scandalous instance of immorality had arisen, in
that one of the members of the congregation was having
sexual relations with his stepmother. The most shameful aspect
of the affair was that so far no steps had been taken to punish
the offender and that the other members of the church had not
allowed it to disturb their own complacency and self-satisfaction. Paul insists that the man must be expelled from the
community.

1. To the Jews this sort of union would be wrong because
it was forbidden by the Law of Moses (Lev. 18: 8). It was also
immorality such as even pagans do not tolerate. It was prohibited
under Roman law, and even though this may not have been
in force in Corinth, public opinion was probably on the same
side.

2. The Corinthians' attitude of complacent toleration may
have been due to the fact that they regarded themselves as in
principle free from the restrictions imposed by a code of moral
behaviour (see 6: 12–20). It is also just possible that if the
offender had previously been a pagan convert to Judaism (before he became a Christian) he might have found a rather over-
ingenious excuse for his conduct in the teaching of the rabbis.
They maintained that when a person accepted the Jewish faith

he broke completely with all previous family ties. The man might therefore have argued that after his earlier conversion to Judaism had taken place the woman who had been his stepmother was such no longer, and that he was perfectly free to contract a union with her if he wished.

3–5. As he writes these sentences Paul is thinking of the congregational meeting at which his letter will be read. Since his instructions, in his own actual words, will be made known to the congregation, he can imagine himself to be *present in spirit*. But it is not only Paul who will be invisibly present. They meet *in the name* of the *Lord Jesus*, and therefore Jesus himself is also with them (see Matt. 18: 20), and it is his *power* which will make the sentence passed upon the offender effective.

5. The man who has committed incest is to be *consigned to Satan for the destruction of the body*. The world in general was thought of as being to some extent under the control of Satan (compare the ideas in 2: 6–8). We see this in the accounts of the temptation of Jesus in Luke and Matthew, where Satan is represented as offering him 'dominion' over 'all the kingdoms of the world', saying, 'for it has been put in my hands' (Luke 4: 5–6). Within the Christian community, however, the kingdom of God was fully established and Christians were under God's protection. To expel someone from the Church was to thrust him out from the sphere within which God ruled and protected his own people into the area of existence where the powers of evil were at large and active. One of Satan's functions was the infliction of pain and disease, as we see from the Book of Job (Job 2: 7), so the result of excommunication will be physical suffering for the offender. But this is intended to be a means of bringing him to his senses, so that he may repent, and may be *saved on the Day of the Lord*.

6–7. Perhaps some of the Corinthians were excusing their failure to take action by pleading that this affair was only an isolated instance of immorality. It was not typical of the congregation as a whole. Paul retorts that even if only one member of the church is involved his conduct will rapidly influence the rest, just as only a very small amount of yeast is necessary to leaven a large lump of dough. The use of this simile reminds him of the Jewish *Passover*. It was the custom, on the day before the festival, to remove every scrap of yeast from the house with great care. The bread eaten during the festival was made without yeast, to commemorate the fact that the Hebrews had escaped from Egypt in haste, taking with them the dough they were baking before it had risen (Deut. 16: 3; Exod. 12: 33–4). He urges his correspondents to remove every trace of moral evil from their community life with equal care. Then they will be *unleavened* in a metaphorical sense, i.e. free from evil influences, just as the Passover bread was unleavened in the literal sense, i.e. free from yeast. The use of leaven as a symbol for evil influence is found also in one of the sayings of Jesus (Matt. 16: 6, 12).

7–8. The reference to the *Passover* leads on to the idea that the Christian life is like a Passover festival all the time. To the Jews the killing of the Passover lamb was meant to remind them of the deliverance of their ancestors from slavery in Egypt at the time of the Exodus. To the Christians the death of Christ was likewise a Passover *sacrifice*. It has rescued men and women not from political tyranny but from the power of death and the domination of sin. Jesus was restored to life, and his resurrection will eventually bring about our own restoration to life (15: 22). As a result of his death we receive God's forgiveness and can make a fresh start, without being discouraged by the memory of what our past life has been like.

9–11. See pp. 3, 8, 12–13. If the contents of this *letter* had been genuinely misunderstood they would certainly have caused considerable anxiety. Many of the congregation would be either slaves in pagan households or workmen in business enterprises owned and managed by non-Christians. They would lose their jobs if they took absolutely literally the injunction to *have nothing to do with* people who were leading

immoral lives. Paul therefore finds it necessary to explain
that he only meant they were to boycott any professing
Christian who was for example a *drunkard* or a *swindler*. A
man of this kind was to be expelled from the church. ✳

CHRISTIANS AND LAWSUITS

6 If one of your number has a dispute with another, has
he the face to take it to pagan law-courts instead of to the
2 community of God's people? It is God's people who are
to judge the world; surely you know that. And if the
world is to come before you for judgement, are you
3 incompetent to deal with these trifling cases? Are you not
aware that we are to judge angels? How much more,
4 mere matters of business! If therefore you have such
business disputes, how can you entrust jurisdiction to
outsiders, men who count for nothing in our community?
5 I write this to shame you. Can it be that there is not a single
wise man among you able to give a decision in a brother-
6 Christian's cause? Must brother go to law with brother
7 —and before unbelievers? Indeed, you already fall below
your standard in going to law with one another at all.
Why not rather suffer injury? Why not rather let your-
8 self be robbed? So far from this, you actually injure and
9 rob—injure and rob your brothers! Surely you know
that the unjust will never come into possession of the
kingdom of God. Make no mistake: no fornicator or
idolater, none who are guilty either of adultery or of
10 homosexual perversion, no thieves or grabbers or
drunkards or slanderers or swindlers, will possess the
11 kingdom of God. Such were some of you. But you have
been through the purifying waters; you have been dedi-

cated to God and justified through the name of the Lord Jesus and the Spirit of our God.

✻ Some of the Corinthians have a regrettable tendency to engage in lawsuits with their fellow-Christians. This is wrong for two reasons. First, they ought not to find it necessary to resort to *pagan* magistrates to settle their *business disputes* with each other. They should be capable of doing this for themselves. Secondly, they ought not to be insisting in such an assertive way on getting their rights.

2–3. It is a much more exacting task *to judge the world* and *to judge angels* than to settle the *trifling cases* which arise in the course of everyday life. Since Christians are eventually to be called upon to perform the more difficult function, they should obviously be able to cope with the easier one. The idea that *God's people...are to judge the world* is probably derived from the similar Jewish belief that the 'saints', i.e. the people of God, and the 'righteous' will share God's own sovereignty over the rest of the world. God will delegate his authority to them and give them dominion over all the nations. We find this idea in the Book of Daniel: 'And the kingdom and the dominion, and the greatness of the kingdoms under the whole heaven, shall be given to the people of the saints of the Most High' (Dan. 7: 27). Who are the *angels*? Possibly they are the 'governing powers' of whom Paul has spoken already (2: 6, 8), supernatural beings who were not originally created evil but who are at the present time opposed to Christ. They may be identical in Paul's mind with the folk-angels whom the Jews of this period believed in. They were angels appointed by God as guardians of the various nations of the world. It was their duty to obey him, but they were able to disobey if they chose. Since the nations they had charge of were frequently hostile to the Jews, God's chosen people, it looked as though most of them were disobedient.

7. This verse recalls the teaching of Jesus, recorded in the Sermon on the Mount: 'Do not set yourself against the man

43

who wrongs you.....If a man wants to sue you for your shirt,
let him have your coat as well' (Matt. 5: 39, 40).

8–10. Here we have a final stern warning to those who
have been provoking the lawsuits by defrauding their fellow-
Christians. People who behave in this way, or who indulge
in the other forms of vice mentioned, *will never come into
possession of the kingdom of God*. This seems to be a comprehensive expression for the enjoyment of the final glorious state
of existence to which Paul and his correspondents looked
forward, a state in which life was eternal and evil of all kinds
had been overcome and destroyed.

11. Some readers of the letter might perhaps become too
severely discouraged by what has just been said, remembering
what kind of lives they had led before they became Christians.
They are reminded that fundamentally they are no longer
what they were before. They *have been through the purifying
waters*. This means that they have been baptized. For Paul the
sacrament of baptism was the beginning of an entirely new
kind of life, of a totally different moral quality (see Rom. 6:
1–14). They *have been dedicated to God*, that is, they have
become members of the community which belongs to God
(see 1: 2) and which must therefore aim at the holiness
characteristic of God himself. They are also *justified*. Their
previous sins have been forgiven so that they need not fear
God's final condemnation, but may hope to be pronounced
'just', i.e. innocent, when the judgement takes place. This
membership of God's holy people and this forgiveness are
gifts granted to them at their baptism, which was a rite
performed in *the name of the Lord Jesus* and at which converts
received the power of *the Spirit*. Here we see a further function of the Spirit of God. It is through the power of the
Spirit that Christians are able to live the new life of moral
goodness which their baptism involves. ✳

CHRISTIANS AND PROSTITUTION

'I am free to do anything', you say. Yes, but not every- 12
thing is for my good. No doubt I am free to do anything,
but I for one will not let anything make free with me.
'Food is for the belly and the belly for food', you say. 13
True; and one day God will put an end to both. But it is
not true that the body is for lust; it is for the Lord—and
the Lord for the body. God not only raised our Lord 14
from the dead; he will also raise us by his power. Do you 15
not know that your bodies are limbs and organs of
Christ? Shall I then take from Christ his bodily parts and
make them over to a harlot? Never! You surely know 16
that anyone who links himself with a harlot becomes
physically one with her (for Scripture says, 'The pair shall
become one flesh'); but he who links himself with Christ 17
is one with him, spiritually. Shun fornication. Every 18
other sin that a man can commit is outside the body;
but the fornicator sins against his own body. Do you 19
not know that your body is a shrine of the indwelling
Holy Spirit, and the Spirit is God's gift to you? You do
not belong to yourselves; you were bought at a price. 20
Then honour God in your body.

* Some members of the church apparently regarded themselves as *free* to have dealings with prostitutes. They are
justifying their conduct by appealing either to a misunderstood
version of Paul's own teaching or else to the ideas current in
popular philosophy. Paul insists that their behaviour is
wrong. He states or implies a number of reasons which
cannot be easily summarized but need to be examined point
by point.

12. The first claim the Corinthians make is: '*I am free to do*

anything'. In opposition to many of the Jewish Christians,
Paul strenuously maintained that Gentile converts to Christianity were under no obligation to attempt to practise all the
detailed religious and moral regulations of the Law of Moses.
This attitude could be misinterpreted to mean that Christians
need not consider themselves bound by any moral restraints
upon their conduct at all. At this stage in the argument the
answer is simply that, granted the principle of freedom of
action, not all kinds of behaviour are beneficial. Also, one
may allow oneself to become enslaved to certain habits so that
one cannot give them up even if one wishes to do so. In that
case one is no longer truly free.

13. The second plea is: '*Food is for the belly and the belly for
food*'. In other words, if we apply the proverb to the matter
in hand, gratification of the sexual instinct, whenever the need
arises, is just as legitimate and just as natural an action as eating
food whenever one is hungry. Some philosophers, believing
that one should live in accordance with Nature and that no
natural function was shameful, applied their philosophical
principles in this way. But there may be a further idea present
as well. This is hinted at in Paul's comment, which seems to
carry on his correspondents' line of thought: *True; and one day
God will put an end to both*. They would say that the physical
body is in any case destined to perish with all its functions, so
that it really matters very little what use we make of them.
The underlying notion is that the soul and the body are two
completely separate things, the one unaffected by the other.
The immortal soul is the real, essential personality, the real self.
For the time being it is encased in the physical body as though
in a prison or a tomb, but it has no fundamental connexion
with it. Therefore, what we do with our physical bodies makes
no difference to our immortal souls which are our real selves.

13–20. The basis of Paul's answer to this point of view is
the Jewish idea of what the real self is. Although man had a
spiritual as well as a physical side to his nature, the Jews did
not suppose that his soul could be clearly isolated or de-

tached from his body. It could not be regarded as the essential person in itself. To the Jew the real person was a combination of spirit, mind, emotions, and physical body, and each of these was affected by all the others. Physical actions had psychological consequences, and vice versa. In the same way we know today that mental illness can show itself by producing physical symptoms. It is also a common fact of experience that physical pain of any sort is apt to affect our general mood and outlook on life. Therefore, when Jews (and Christians) thought of the restoration of the human personality after death, they spoke of a bodily resurrection. The human self will need some form of bodily expression in the future life, just as we now require our bodies for self-expression—our physical brains to think with, our vocal chords to express our thoughts in speech, and so on. And the self which is to be restored to life will be the self which has been previously formed and shaped and influenced by its life in the physical body here on earth.

The specific points made in answer to the Corinthians' attitude to fornication are as follows.

(i) The body does not exist merely to perform purely physical functions within the sphere of the natural world: *it is for the Lord*. It is the instrument of a personality related to Christ, and Christ now lives in a sphere beyond the present material world. It exists in order that the human person may carry out the commands of Christ.

(ii) The *Lord* is *for the body*. The body is not something inessential and unimportant by comparison with the immortal soul. It is an aspect of human nature about which Christ himself is concerned.

(iii) *God not only raised our Lord from the dead; he will also raise us by his power*. It is the human personality which has been shaped by its physical existence on earth which is eventually to be restored to life. What we do here and now in this physical world is going to make a vital difference to our eternal destiny.

47

(iv) Christians are so closely related to Christ that they can be described as limbs of his body (see chapter 12), *his bodily parts*. This means that *he who links himself with Christ is one with him, spiritually*. The character and personality of Christ himself is in some way transmitted to his followers as a result of this relationship. Now Paul maintains that when sexual intercourse takes place between a man and a woman there is likewise a union of two personalities. It is not merely a passing physical act with no permanent consequences for the real selves of the people concerned, it is something which has a lasting psychological and spiritual effect. Each person shares his or her character with the other. The fact that a man who has intercourse with a prostitute *becomes physically one with her* means that his whole personality is united with hers, and that her character becomes his. And since, to Paul's mind, a prostitute was necessarily a woman of evil character, it follows that the man becomes morally corrupted. Thus, his spiritual connexion with Christ is broken, since he cannot at one and the same time share the character of Christ and the character of an evil personality. It has been suggested that the prostitutes in question may perhaps have been sacred prostitutes employed in the temple of Aphrodite, the Greek goddess of love. Intercourse with these women was thought to effect union with the goddess herself. If this suggestion is correct, it lends additional force to the assertion that union with a prostitute destroys the union of the Christian with Christ. At a later point in the letter Paul claims that although the pagan deities have no real existence as gods they nevertheless represent demonic spiritual powers who are hostile to Christ (10: 18–22). In that case, intercourse with a cult prostitute would not only be a matter of exposing oneself to an evil moral influence on the purely human plane. It would also put one in contact with the powers of evil themselves, and place one in the ranks of Christ's enemies.

(v) The body of a Christian is like a temple, since God himself is present within the Christian personality by means of *the indwelling Holy Spirit*. Therefore, intimate contact with an evil character is like desecrating a temple.

(vi) In reply to the claim of absolute individual freedom made by his correspondents, Paul points out that this is not a true picture of the situation. They do not belong to themselves. They are like slaves *bought* by Christ, and so are not free to disregard his commands.

(vii) *Every other sin that a man can commit is outside the body; but the fornicator sins against his own body*. This verse presents difficulties. If the word *body* here is taken in the purely physical sense the first half of the statement is plainly incorrect. There are most certainly other sins that are committed by means of the physical body and have detrimental physical effects, sins such as drunkenness and gluttony (we might ourselves add drug addiction to the list). These sins could not be spoken of as *outside the body*. It is often suggested that *body* is to be taken as meaning 'personality', but it is not immediately clear that this provides a more helpful answer. It is not only fornication that has a fundamentally corrupting effect upon the inner personality. Idolatry would be just as effective in severing the spiritual connexion of the Christian with Christ. The least unsatisfactory solution seems to be to take *body* in the sense of 'personality', to omit the word '*other*' in the first part of the verse (it does not appear in the original Greek), and to suppose that this first half should be put into inverted commas as a claim which Paul's opponents are making. They say that whatever sin a man may commit, whether it be fornication or indulgence in some other form of vice, it is *outside*, i.e. nothing to do with, his real personality. Paul replies (in the second half of verse 18) that, on the contrary, a man who commits fornication is after all doing some vital damage to his essential self. ✻

The Christian in a Pagan Society

PROBLEMS OF MARRIAGE AND DIVORCE

7 AND NOW FOR the matters you wrote about.
It is a good thing for a man to have nothing to do
2 with women; but because there is so much immorality,
let each man have his own wife and each woman her own
3 husband. The husband must give the wife what is due
to her, and the wife equally must give the husband his
4 due. The wife cannot claim her body as her own; it is her
husband's. Equally, the husband cannot claim his body
5 as his own; it is his wife's. Do not deny yourselves to
one another, except when you agree upon a temporary
abstinence in order to devote yourselves to prayer; afterwards you may come together again; otherwise, for lack
of self-control, you may be tempted by Satan.

6, 7 All this I say by way of concession, not command. I
should like you all to be as I am myself; but everyone has
the gift God has granted him, one this gift and another
that.

8 To the unmarried and to widows I say this: it is a good
9 thing if they stay as I am myself; but if they cannot control themselves, they should marry. Better be married
than burn with vain desire.

10 To the married I give this ruling, which is not mine but
the Lord's: a wife must not separate herself from her
11 husband; if she does, she must either remain unmarried
or be reconciled to her husband; and the husband must not
divorce his wife.

To the rest I say this, as my own word, not as the 12
Lord's: if a Christian has a heathen wife, and she is willing
to live with him, he must not divorce her; and a woman 13
who has a heathen husband willing to live with her must
not divorce her husband. For the heathen husband now 14
belongs to God through his Christian wife, and the
heathen wife through her Christian husband. Otherwise
your children would not belong to God, whereas in fact
they do. If on the other hand the heathen partner wishes 15
for a separation, let him have it. In such cases the Christian
husband or wife is under no compulsion; but God's call
is a call to live in peace. Think of it: as a wife you may 16
be your husband's salvation; as a husband you may be your
wife's salvation.

* It appears that the Corinthians themselves had consulted
Paul about various problems of Christian behaviour (see
p. 11). It is to these topics that he now turns his attention.
The attitude of mind he displays throughout chapter 7 will
probably seem uncongenial to us. If we are to understand it,
we shall have to remember that he expected the world as we
know it to come to an end very shortly. This partly accounts
for what he says about marriage and about slavery.

1–5. Some married members of the congregation have
been refusing physical intercourse to their husbands or wives.
It may be that conversion to Christianity had brought with
it such a revulsion of feeling against the evil sexual habits
of the pagan population of Corinth that this had led to the
belief that physical relations within marriage itself were evil.
Furthermore, the sort of philosophy which made a complete
separation between the immortal soul (the essential personality) and the physical body, while it might encourage sexual
licence (see 6: 13), might also lead to an equally wrong insistence on sexual abstinence. The immortal soul was thought

to be the only part of oneself which could be thought of as morally good. It would then follow that all physical functions were in themselves evil, and that one must refrain from exercising them as far as was humanly possible. Paul's answer is, first, that this kind of behaviour is selfish. Married people belong to each other, and it is not for one partner to pursue some form of individual self-discipline in disregard of the other person's needs. *The wife cannot claim her body as her own; it is her husband's. Equally, the husband cannot claim his body as his own; it is his wife's.* Secondly, it is dangerous. The partner who has been refused intercourse will, *for lack of self-control*, look elsewhere for satisfaction. If the physical relationship is to be discontinued at all, it must be only *a temporary abstinence*, agreed upon by both partners in order that they may *devote* themselves *to prayer* for a certain space of time. This was an idea found in some of the pagan religious cults. Jewish Christians would also be aware that the same habit was encouraged in Judaism on the Day of Atonement.

1, 6–9. Despite his sound advice to those who are already married, it is obvious that Paul himself thinks it preferable to remain unmarried. Marriage, in his view, is only for those who are unable to deny themselves the physical satisfaction which it allows: *Better be married than burn with vain desire.* This no doubt seems a very negative view. If, however, one supposes that this present earthly life is to end in the immediate future, there is little point in thinking in a more positive way of marriage as lifelong companionship and the means of founding and bringing up a family.

10–11. We turn now to the question of divorce. In a situation where both partners are Christian the teaching of Jesus himself can be applied without any difficulty (see Mark 10: 1–12).

12–16. When Jesus spoke about divorce he was talking to Jews who had Jewish wives who shared their own religious beliefs, in the same way that a Christian husband and a Christian wife share their beliefs. Where this does not hold good, i.e. if a Christian is married to a non-Christian, some practical modification of Jesus' teaching is necessary. In this case, the Christian partner is not to attempt to prolong the marriage against the will of the unbelieving partner. *If...the heathen partner wishes for a separation*, then divorce is allowable. Some commentators maintain that when Paul says that in circumstances such as these *the Christian husband or wife is under no compulsion* he means that he or she is also at liberty to marry again. Nevertheless, if the non-Christian is willing to continue the marriage, the Christian partner must not take the initiative in asking for a divorce. If we suppose that 2 Cor. 6: 14 — 7: 1 is part of the earlier letter referred to in I Cor. 5: 9 we might suggest that the warning found there against marriage to unbelievers had caused some Christians already married to heathen partners to wonder whether divorce was not only allowable but a positive duty. In any case the question would arise quite naturally. The early Christians were conscious of the fact that as God's people they were in some way separate from the rest of the world and that it was their duty to remain so. Some will have asked how this state of separation could be maintained when at the same time they shared the most intimate of human relationships with husbands or wives who were not themselves Christians.

Paul's answer is that a marriage of this kind does not in fact hinder the separation of the Christian community from the world at large. The non-Christian partner himself (or herself) belongs to God's people by virtue of the marriage relationship. *For the heathen husband now belongs to God through his Christian wife, and the heathen wife through her Christian husband.* This is probably based on the idea which we find in the Old Testament that the family as a whole is like a single personality. What happens to one member of the family happens to all the other members as well, and what one member does he does representatively on behalf of the whole family, so that they are all involved in the consequences, whether good or bad. (There is an example of this in Josh. 7. Achan stole forbidden booty from the ruins of Jericho, and his family were all put to death with him, being considered equally guilty of the crime he had committed.) The point is underlined here by an appeal to one aspect of family solidarity which the readers of the letter apparently took for granted, the fact that their children also belonged to God's people. If this is true of the children of a Christian it must be true also of a non-Christian married to a believer. This idea is not to be taken to extremes, however. It does not mean that the unbelieving partner will automatically share in the final destiny which belongs to Christians whether or not he or she is personally converted to the faith. His *salvation* is only a possibility, not a certainty. Ultimately it depends upon his own personal decision. ✳

THE INSIGNIFICANCE OF SOCIAL AND RACIAL DISTINCTIONS

17 However that may be, each one must order his life according to the gift the Lord has granted him and his condition when God called him. That is what I teach in
18 all our congregations. Was a man called with the marks of circumcision on him? Let him not remove them. Was he uncircumcised when he was called? Let him not
19 be circumcised. Circumcision or uncircumcision is neither here nor there; what matters is to keep God's commands.
20 Every man should remain in the condition in which he
21 was called. Were you a slave when you were called? Do not let that trouble you; but if a chance of liberty
22 should come, take it. For the man who as a slave received the call to be a Christian is the Lord's freedman, and, equally, the free man who received the call is a slave
23 in the service of Christ. You were bought at a price;

do not become slaves of men. Thus each one, my friends, 24
is to remain before God in the condition in which he
received his call.

* This is something of a digression from the main theme of
the chapter. The basic point is that Christians must not
attempt to make any fundamental change in their circumstances as a result of their conversion.

18. *Was a man called with the marks of circumcision on him?
Let him not remove them.* This is perhaps a hypothetical example,
rather than something which was actually happening in
Corinth. It does not seem very likely that Jewish Christians
would attempt to disguise the physical signs of their Jewish
origin. (This had actually been done by some young Jews
in Jerusalem in the time of Antiochus Epiphanes, the King
of Syria (175–164 B.C.) who ruled Palestine and tried to
abolish the Jewish religion. Wishing to adopt Greek ways of
life, including the custom of engaging in athletic exercises
completely naked, they submitted to a surgical operation to
conceal the fact that they had been circumcised. But there is
no obvious reason why the Corinthians should have followed
their example.) *Was he uncircumcised when he was called? Let
him not be circumcised.* It is more likely that there were Gentile
Christians who were inclined to wonder whether, if they were
to belong to God's people in the fullest possible way, they
ought not to submit to the rite of circumcision which had been
in the past the outward sign of membership of God's chosen
race, the Jews. It was a question about which Paul himself held
very firm convictions, as we can see from his letter to the
churches of Galatia. To accept circumcision is there presented
as a complete denial of the Christian faith. Here his attitude is
milder (it may be that this was not a very urgent problem in
Corinth). Circumcision is merely an external physical condition which has in itself no importance at all (verse 19).

21–3. The question of slavery is obviously a real one. To
us it is surprising that slavery appears to be accepted without

protest as part of the recognized order of society. Again, however, if one expects the world shortly to come to an end, long-term programmes of social reform are beside the point.

But the reason given here for the advice not to worry about being a *slave* is rather different. It is simply that one's social status in this world has no bearing at all upon one's position as a Christian and one's relationship to Christ. Christ has set his followers free from a kind of slavery much more fundamental and important than slavery in the literal sense. He has rescued them from the domination of evil. Therefore, the Christian slave is truly set free. He *is the Lord's freedman*. His position in society is reversed within the Church. If he has a Christian master, his legal status no longer matters, even though he may formally continue to be a slave. This is illustrated by Paul's letter to Philemon, a Christian at Colossae, about one of Philemon's slaves (Onesimus) who had run away and had later met Paul in prison and been converted by him. He says: 'For perhaps this is why you lost him for a time, that you might have him back for good, no longer as a slave, but as more than a slave—as a dear brother, very dear indeed to me and how much dearer to you, both as man and as Christian' (Philem. 15-16). The position of the free citizen who has become a Christian is also reversed. He is *a slave in the service of Christ*, under the control of a master who has the absolute right of disposing of his time and his powers as he thinks fit. Christians must therefore no longer pay attention to purely human ideas about rank and status: *do not become slaves of men.* ✳

CELIBACY

25 On the question of celibacy, I have no instructions from the Lord, but I give my judgement as one who by God's mercy is fit to be trusted.

26 It is my opinion, then, that in a time of stress like the present this is the best way for a man to live—it is best for

a man to be as he is. Are you bound in marriage? Do 27
not seek a dissolution. Has your marriage been dissolved?
Do not seek a wife. If, however, you do marry, there is 28
nothing wrong in it; and if a virgin marries, she has done
no wrong. But those who marry will have pain and grief
in this bodily life, and my aim is to spare you.

What I mean, my friends, is this. The time we live in 29
will not last long. While it lasts, married men should be
as if they had no wives; mourners should be as if they 30
had nothing to grieve them, the joyful as if they did not
rejoice; buyers must not count on keeping what they buy,
nor those who use the world's wealth on using it to the 31
full. For the whole frame of this world is passing away.

I want you to be free from anxious care. The un- 32
married man cares for the Lord's business; his aim is to
please the Lord. But the married man cares for worldly 33
things; his aim is to please his wife; and he has a divided 34
mind. The unmarried or celibate woman cares for the
Lord's business; her aim is to be dedicated to him in body
as in spirit; but the married woman cares for worldly
things; her aim is to please her husband.

In saying this I have no wish to keep you on a tight rein. 35
I am thinking simply of your own good, of what is
seemly, and of your freedom to wait upon the Lord
without distraction.

But if a man has a partner in celibacy and feels that he 36
is not behaving properly towards her, if, that is, his in-
stincts are too strong for him, and something must be
done, he may do as he pleases; there is nothing wrong in
it; let them marry. But if a man is steadfast in his purpose, 37
being under no compulsion, and has complete control of

his own choice; and if he has decided in his own mind
to preserve his partner in her virginity, he will do well.

38 Thus, he who marries his partner does well, and he who
does not will do better.

39 A wife is bound to her husband as long as he lives. But
if the husband die, she is free to marry whom she will,
provided the marriage is within the Lord's fellowship.

40 But she is better off as she is; that is my opinion, and
I believe that I too have the Spirit of God.

✶ Paul goes on to explain in more detail his reasons for
thinking it preferable to remain unmarried. They are these.

If one is still single, it is better not to embark on married
life, simply because *The time we live in will not last long*
(verse 29). There is therefore no point in making any significant change in one's ordinary way of life. This leads to a short
digression (verses 29–31) on the general advisability of adopting a detached attitude towards all present earthly experiences.
Paul's words here are not to be understood in their absolutely
literal sense, otherwise his advice that *married men should be as
if they had no wives* would obviously contradict what he has
said earlier (verses 3–5). He probably means that if one
becomes too much involved in the occupations and relationships of daily life one will be unprepared for the moment of
judgement when this present world comes to an end.

Secondly, *those who marry will have pain and grief in this
bodily life* (verse 28). Both Jews and Christians thought
that the period of time immediately before the end of the
world would be a time of unprecedented calamity and
disaster (*a time of stress*). There would be wars, earthquakes,
and famines, and the Temple in Jerusalem would be dese-
crated (see Mark 13: 7, 8, 14–20). In particular it would be a
time of hardship and sorrow for women with babies and for
expectant mothers. Paul extends this idea to include all those
with family ties, both men and women. Presumably the point

is that they will have to endure not only their own individual sufferings but also the pain and grief of seeing husbands, wives, or children suffer as well.

Lastly, according to Paul's way of thinking, a married person is more preoccupied with *worldly things*, the material needs of his or her family, and is therefore less at liberty to care for *the Lord's business* (a rather vague expression, perhaps the equivalent of our 'church work'). Also, someone who is married is chiefly concerned to *please* his or her partner, and this distracts one from aiming wholeheartedly at pleasing Christ (verses 32–4).

36–8. Despite all that has been said about the advantages of remaining single, we are not to suppose that there is anything wrong in marriage. Even if a man has taken some kind of a vow of celibacy, it is still permissible for him to marry, should he find that he is after all unfitted for the celibate life. The situation pictured here is apparently that of a man and a woman who have decided to live with each other without marrying and having sexual intercourse. The motive behind this somewhat impracticable arrangement may perhaps have been an attempt to anticipate here on earth the future resurrection existence in which marriage as such would be no more (see Mark 12: 25). In principle Paul approves of the idea, but in practice he realizes the difficulties, and is careful to reassure the men and women concerned that it is no sin for them to marry if they find the situation too much for them. Readers of the N.E.B. who are familiar with the A.V. and R.V. will notice that the A.V. and R.V. give a quite different description of the problem which is being dealt with in the verses we are considering. These versions give the impression that Paul is discussing the question of whether or not a father should allow his daughter to marry. It is true that he expresses himself rather obscurely, and that the Greek could be made to fit this interpretation (it is offered as an alternative in the footnotes in the N.E.B.). But the version given in the text of the N.E.B. is the better one, for at least two reasons. First, if Paul is really talking about a man and his daughter it is strange that he should use the word 'virgin' (*parthenos*, translated here as *partner in celibacy*) instead of the ordinary and usual Greek word for 'daughter' (*thugater*). Secondly, what is said in verse 37, about the man's being *steadfast in his purpose...under no compulsion*, and possessing sufficient willpower to carry out his decision, is surely very odd and very extravagantly expressed if it is a question merely of a father deciding whether or not to give his daughter in marriage. Why should he be under any compulsion one way or the other? And why should such strength of will be necessary in order to refuse to do so? ✷

IDOL MEAT

8 Now about food consecrated to heathen deities.

Of course we all 'have knowledge', as you say. This
2 'knowledge' breeds conceit; it is love that builds. If anyone fancies that he knows, he knows nothing yet,
3 in the true sense of knowing. But if a man loves, he is acknowledged by God.

4 Well then, about eating this consecrated food: of course, as you say, 'a false god has no existence in the real
5 world. There is no god but one.' For indeed, if there be so-called gods, whether in heaven or on earth—as indeed
6 there are many 'gods' and many 'lords'—yet for us there is one God, the Father, from whom all being comes, to-wards whom we move; and there is one Lord, Jesus Christ, through whom all things came to be, and we through him.

7 But not everyone knows this. There are some who have been so accustomed to idolatry that even now they eat this food with a sense of its heathen consecration, and their conscience, being weak, is polluted by the eating.
8 Certainly food will not bring us into God's presence: if

we do not eat, we are none the worse, and if we eat, we
are none the better. But be careful that this liberty of 9
yours does not become a pitfall for the weak. If a weak 10
character sees you sitting down to a meal in a heathen
temple—you, who 'have knowledge'—will not his
conscience be emboldened to eat food consecrated to
the heathen deity? This 'knowledge' of yours is utter 11
disaster to the weak, the brother for whom Christ died.
In thus sinning against your brothers and wounding their 12
conscience, you sin against Christ. And therefore, if food 13
be the downfall of my brother, I will never eat meat any
more, for I will not be the cause of my brother's downfall.

✶ The problem of *food consecrated to heathen deities* was one
which all Christians in Corinth would frequently encounter.
The city was full of pagan temples where animal sacrifices
were offered to the gods, and there were several ways
in which one might find oneself involved in eating food
which had its origin in these pagan sacrifices. The meat
sold in the ordinary shops frequently came from the temples.
Priests and worshippers at a sacrifice would ceremonially eat
part of the animal and then the rest of the carcass would
be disposed of by selling it to the butchers. Even if
Christians were scrupulous enough to make sure that the
meat they themselves bought had not been obtained in this
way, they might well have non-Christian friends. If their
friends invited them to dinner the food provided would
probably be idol meat. Also, they might belong to some
kind of trade guild which would have an annual banquet,
held in one of the temples, after a sacrifice in honour of
the god who was the 'patron saint' of the guild. The food for
the banquet would come from the sacrificed animal. It was
possibly difficult for Christians to absent themselves from
such functions entirely. They would therefore find themselves
confronted with the question of whether or not it was sinful

to eat consecrated food. Was it a form of idolatry? Or was it after all a matter of no importance? It looks as though there was a difference of opinion in Corinth. At any rate, they had written to ask Paul for advice about it. In principle he agrees with the more liberal members of the congregation that there is nothing wrong in eating food of this kind. But he warns them that they must not entirely disregard the scruples of those who take the narrower view.

2–3. He begins by stating the basic principle which should govern the discussion of ethical problems: *love*, that is, genuine consideration for the welfare of the other person, is more fundamental in the Christian life than the *knowledge* upon which the more enlightened Corinthians were basing their line of action. It is *if a man loves* that he is recognized by God as belonging to him.

4–6. The liberal and enlightened Christians argue that '*a false god has no existence in the real world*'. Therefore, since the idol to which the animal has been offered is not really a god at all, the sacrifice has no religious meaning. The food from the animal remains ordinary food, and there is no reason why a Christian should refuse to eat it on grounds of conscience. Paul is bound to admit that there is a good deal of truth in this. The pagan '*gods*', often addressed by the title of '*lord*', are only *so-called*. They are not real deities, whatever their supposed character and attributes. (The ones *in heaven* would include the Greek gods and goddesses such as Zeus, Apollo, Aphrodite and Pallas Athene, and also foreign deities such as the Egyptian Osiris and Isis. The ones *on earth* would be kings, who in the East were often revered as divine during their lifetime, and also famous men, such as Heracles, who were thought to have become gods after their death.) There is in reality only *one God*, who has created the whole universe. It is this God *towards whom we move*. The eventual destiny of the whole human race, and each separate member of it, is life with God. For Christians there is also only *one Lord, Jesus Christ*. The use of the title *Lord* shows that the early Christians worshipped Jesus as a divine being. The word was used in the Greek-speaking world with reference to the gods, and it occurs in the Septuagint as the title of God himself. Jesus' followers were convinced that after his resurrection he had in some mysterious way entered God's own sphere of existence in heaven (see the narrative of the Ascension in Acts 1: 6–11), and that he now shared the powers and functions of God. They gradually came to believe also that if he now shared the status of God himself he must always have done so from the very beginning. Paul can therefore say that it is Christ *through whom all things came to be*. Christ assisted God in the work of creating the universe, including ourselves (*and we through him*).

These two fundamental beliefs expressed in verse 6 may well seem to contradict each other. How can Christ be divine if there is only one God? Alternatively, if Christians are right to worship Christ as divine this surely leads to belief in two gods—and, if two, why not many more, i.e. the *many 'gods' and many 'lords'* of the pagan world? All that can be said here is that the early Church did not in fact see any inconsistency in what they believed about God and what they believed about Christ. This may have been due simply to a failure to think logically about their faith. There may on the other hand be a more profound reason. Our human minds can never completely and fully understand the nature of God. Our knowledge of him is bound to be fragmentary and incomplete. We may partially comprehend several different aspects of his character, but his being as a whole eludes our human powers of description and definition. Because of this, some of the things we say about him may at the same time be perfectly true and yet may appear to be inconsistent with each other, as when we say that there is only one God and also that Christ shares the divine character and status. In so far as we can attempt, with our human limitations, to resolve the inconsistency, we can do so only by referring to the doctrine of the Trinity (finally formulated several centuries after the writing of the New Testament). The one God exists, eternally and simultaneously, in three different modes of being, as Father, as Son, and as Holy Spirit, so that within the being of God himself there are what we think of as personal relationships. As Son, God experienced our own human life in the person of Jesus of Nazareth. It follows that Christ is not a second god, but God himself in one of his modes of existence.

7–13. In principle the enlightened members of the congregation are right. But their position nevertheless contains certain weaknesses. For one thing, they seem to suppose that it is a positive virtue to insist upon their liberty of action and to make a point of eating idol meat, as though God thought the better of them for doing so. This is not true. *Certainly food will not bring us into God's presence*. (The metaphor here is that of the offering of a sacrifice, which was thought to put the worshipper in contact with his god and to secure his god's approval of him.) The mere eating of food is not in itself a morally good action: *if we do not eat, we are none the worse, and if we eat, we are none the better*. Secondly, their actions may have disastrous consequences for fellow-Christians less enlightened than themselves. The possible situation Paul has in mind is this. One of the liberal-minded Christians may be seen *sitting down to a meal in a heathen temple*. Presumably he would be attending a guild banquet, or perhaps a private dinner party given by a friend but held in the temple precincts. Clearly the food would be idol meat. His less enlightened fellow-Christian may temporarily be influenced by his action and may follow his example: *his conscience* will *be emboldened to eat food consecrated to the heathen deity*. But because he has not yet shaken off the strong psychological influence of his pre-Christian outlook and habits, he still thinks of this food as having religious significance. He eats it *with a sense of its heathen consecration* (verse 7); to him it means indulging in the sin of *idolatry*. Therefore his conscience *is polluted by the eating*. His conscience troubles him and makes him feel guilty. We must notice at this point that when Paul speaks of people who have a *weak* conscience he means by this the exact opposite of what we mean ourselves. We use the term of someone who has very few moral scruples and whose conscience is not at all active. Paul uses it of someone who has a great many moral scruples, some of them rather trivial ones. It indicates a person whose conscience is over-active. He is a *weak character* in the present instance because his faith is not sufficiently strong for him to believe wholeheartedly that the idols he previously worshipped do not really exist. The upshot of the whole situation is that the *liberty* of the enlightened Christian has become *a pitfall for the weak*, since he is led to commit what he afterwards believes to be a sin. ✶

APOSTOLIC QUALIFICATIONS AND PRIVILEGES

Am I not a free man? Am I not an apostle? Did I not see **9** Jesus our Lord? Are not you my own handiwork, in the Lord? If others do not accept me as an apostle, you at 2 least are bound to do so, for you are yourselves the very seal of my apostolate, in the Lord.

To those who put me in the dock this is my answer: 3 Have I no right to eat and drink? Have I no right to take 4, 5 a Christian wife about with me, like the rest of the apostles and the Lord's brothers, and Cephas? Or are Barnabas 6 and I alone bound to work for our living? Did you ever 7 hear of a man serving in the army at his own expense? or planting a vineyard without eating the fruit of it? or tending a flock without using its milk? Do not suppose 8 I rely on these human analogies; in the Law of Moses 9 we read, 'A threshing ox shall not be muzzled.' Do you suppose God's concern is with oxen? Or is the reference 10 clearly to ourselves? Of course it refers to us, in the sense

that the ploughman should plough and the thresher thresh
11 in the hope of getting some of the produce. If we have
sown a spiritual crop for you, is it too much to expect
12 from you a material harvest? If you allow others these
rights, have not we a stronger claim?

✳ It has sometimes been suggested that we have here the
beginning of a separate letter, but this view has not been
widely accepted (see pp. 4–5). The chapter as a whole contains
two themes. On the one hand, Paul pursues the idea, found
at the end of chapter 8, that one must do everything possible
to prevent other people from being hindered in their attempts
to live a Christian life. He himself has not claimed his rights
as an apostle, and he tries to adapt himself as far as he can
to the outlook of the people he preaches to. On the other
hand, he remembers that his conduct has been questioned or
misunderstood by his opponents. They have probably accused
him of being uncertain of his position. If he refrains from
claiming the privileges which belong to an apostle, is it
because he knows he is not really entitled to them? He therefore begins by making it quite clear that he does genuinely
possess the qualifications of an apostle.

1. *Am I not a free man?* He himself claims as much liberty
of conscience and of action as his correspondents in Corinth.
He implies that, if he nevertheless chooses to show consideration to the scruples of those who are less enlightened, his
liberal-minded correspondents should do the same.

1–2. *Am I not an apostle?* See 1: 1. Here Paul refers not
only to his basic qualifications for taking up the work of an
apostle but also to the fact that he has in actual practice proved
that this is the task to which God has called him. The very
existence of the Christian church in Corinth is due to the
success of his missionary work. His converts are the *seal* of his
apostolate. A seal, like our trademark, was a guarantee of the
genuineness of the product.

3–6. The privileges to which an apostle is entitled are, first, financial support (or its equivalent in food and lodgings) from the churches he founds and visits, and, secondly, should he be married and should his *wife* accompany him on his journeys, support for his wife as well. Paul implies that this second privilege was taken advantage of by *the rest of the apostles and the Lord's brothers, and Cephas*. We find the names of the brothers of Jesus in Mark 6: 3, James, Joseph, Judas and Simon. We know from John 7: 5 that they were not his followers during his earthly career. Presumably they were converted as a result of his resurrection, and so became apostles. We know that Jesus appeared to James (see 15: 7) and that James became one of the leading apostles in Jerusalem (Gal. 1: 19). Possibly Cephas receives particular mention here because of the Cephas-party in Corinth. Paul is anxious to show them that he himself possesses rights equal to those of their favourite apostle.

8–10. The fact that the apostles may justifiably claim these privileges is substantiated by an appeal to Scripture. In Deut. 25: 4 there is a harvesting regulation which says that the oxen used for threshing are not to be muzzled to prevent them from eating the grain as they trample it down and separate it from the husks. In its context this is of course intended to be taken literally. Paul, however, sees that the regulations about animals in the *Law of Moses* can be understood metaphorically and are to be referred to human beings. He argues that God would not bother to make laws for the benefit of *oxen* only. This rule, therefore, can be applied to the apostles, to show that they have every right to some material return for their missionary labours. ✳

PAUL'S RENUNCIATION OF HIS RIGHTS

But I have availed myself of no such right. On the contrary, I put up with all that comes my way rather than offer any hindrance to the gospel of Christ. You know 13 (do you not?) that those who perform the temple service eat the temple offerings, and those who wait upon the

14 altar claim their share of the sacrifice. In the same way the
Lord gave instructions that those who preach the Gospel
15 should earn their living by the Gospel. But I have never
taken advantage of any such right, nor do I intend to
claim it in this letter. I had rather die! No one shall
16 make my boast an empty boast. Even if I preach the
Gospel, I can claim no credit for it; I cannot help myself;
17 it would be misery to me not to preach. If I did it of my
own choice, I should be earning my pay; but since I do it
apart from my own choice, I am simply discharging a
18 trust. Then what is my pay? The satisfaction of preaching
the Gospel without expense to anyone; in other words, of
waiving the rights which my preaching gives me.

* Now that he has sufficiently established his own right to
apostolic privileges, Paul goes on to explain his various
motives for renouncing them.

12 *b*. The first reason is that he does not wish to *offer any
hindrance to the gospel of Christ*. Perhaps he felt that the life of
most of his converts was difficult enough financially without
his making himself a burden to them and so causing them to be
distracted by problems of money from their devotion to the
service of Christ. Perhaps some of his critics were inclined to
accuse him of actually making a profit out of his missionary
work and he wished to give them no grounds for doing
so. Jewish converts and prospective converts might have
objected to a Christian apostle who took payment for his
teaching, since no Jewish rabbi would do this. Criticism of
Paul's methods might in turn lead to the rejection of the
gospel he preached. To insist on his rights might therefore
hinder his real task.

13–14. He has more to say about the reasons for his
conduct. But first he mentions two further considerations in
support of his fellow-apostles' habit of accepting maintenance

from the churches where they work. Both among Jews and among pagans, the priests who offered *sacrifice* lived on the offerings brought by the worshippers. It may be that Paul is thinking here only of Jewish worship, in which case *those who perform the temple service* are the Levites, who formed the Temple choir and served in a subordinate capacity, and *those who wait upon the altar* are the priests, who actually offered the sacrifices. This is only an analogy or illustration, like those in verse 7. More powerful support for apostolic practice is to be found in a saying of Jesus himself. The reference is probably to the words recorded in Luke 10: 7, where Jesus is represented as giving instructions to the disciples he is sending out on a preaching mission: 'Stay in that one house, sharing their food and drink; for the worker earns his pay.' Their preaching is real work, which entitles them to board and lodging by way of payment.

15. What has been said already is not to be taken as a hint that in the future Paul expects his readers to offer him financial support.

16–18. The other motive for his course of action is rather obscurely expressed. He says that he does not deserve *pay* of any kind for *preaching* about Christ. If this were something he had voluntarily chosen to do, a task which he had undertaken on his own initiative, then he might perhaps *claim* some *credit* for it, and some reward for doing it. But this is not so. He does his work as an apostle under a deep sense of compulsion. Perhaps he is here contrasting his own experience with that of the apostles who had been followers of Jesus during his earthly career. They had willingly accepted Jesus' claims about himself from the very beginning and had willingly become his disciples. Paul, on the other hand, originally had persecuted the Christians, and had himself become a follower of Christ only as a result of what happened to him on the road to Damascus, under compulsion, as it were. He may also be comparing himself with the prophets of previous centuries who likewise felt that they had no choice about their vocation:

'the Lord God hath spoken, who can but prophesy?' (Amos 3: 8). In any case, since he *can claim no credit* for his actual preaching, the only thing he can *boast* about, humanly speaking the only thing for which he deserves *pay* or *credit*, is, paradoxically enough, the fact that he preaches *the Gospel without expense to anyone*. This is the only form of service to Christ which he can offer freely, of his own choice and on his own initiative. And the *satisfaction* of being able to do this is its own reward. ✻

FURTHER EXAMPLES OF PERSONAL RENUNCIATION

19 I am a free man and own no master; but I have made myself every man's servant, to win over as many as
20 possible. To Jews I became like a Jew, to win Jews; as they are subject to the Law of Moses, I put myself under that law to win them although I am not myself subject to it.
21 To win Gentiles, who are outside the Law, I made myself like one of them, although I am not in truth outside God's
22 law, being under the law of Christ. To the weak I became weak, to win the weak. Indeed, I have become everything in turn to men of every sort, so that in one way or
23 another I may save some. All this I do for the sake of the Gospel, to bear my part in proclaiming it.
24 You know (do you not?) that at the sports all the runners run the race, though only one wins the prize.
25 Like them, run to win! But every athlete goes into strict training. They do it to win a fading wreath; we, a wreath
26 that never fades. For my part, I run with a clear goal before me; I am like a boxer who does not beat the air;
27 I bruise my own body and make it know its master, for fear that after preaching to others I should find myself rejected.

✱ Here we have some more illustrations, drawn from Paul's own way of life, of the renunciation of individual preferences in matters of conduct and opinion with the aim of furthering the progress of the Christian faith among others.

20. When trying to convert *Jews*, Paul conformed to the *Law of Moses*, though he did not believe it essential to do so. He had Timothy circumcised, when he met him in Lystra and wanted his help in missionary work (Acts 16: 3).

21. When he was preaching to *Gentiles* Paul would refrain from practising any Jewish customs which they might find strange, and would try to put himself in the same position as his hearers. At Athens he began his sermon by referring to the Athenian altar dedicated 'To an Unknown God', and claimed that both he and the Athenians worshipped the one God, with the difference that the Athenians were ignorant of God's nature and purposes (Acts 17: 22–31).

22. When dealing with the *weak*, i.e. the overscrupulous and immature such as those described in the previous chapter, he was careful to respect conscientious scruples which he did not himself share.

25–7. The foregoing remarks might lend themselves to some misunderstanding and might lead Paul's more critical correspondents to accuse him of being too easy-going and changeable. He insists that on the contrary he has *a clear goal* in front of him, and that like an *athlete* in *training* he practises the strictest self-discipline. ✱

SCRIPTURAL WARNINGS

You should understand, my brothers, that our ancestors **10** were all under the pillar of cloud, and all of them passed through the Red Sea; and so they all received baptism into 2 the fellowship of Moses in cloud and sea. They all ate the 3 same supernatural food, and all drank the same super- 4 natural drink; I mean, they all drank from the supernatural rock that accompanied their travels—and that rock

5 was Christ. And yet, most of them were not accepted by God, for the desert was strewn with their corpses.

6 These events happened as symbols to warn us not to

7 set our desires on evil things, as they did. Do not be idolaters, like some of them; as Scripture has it, 'the

8 people sat down to feast and stood up to play'. Let us not commit fornication, as some of them did—and

9 twenty-three thousand died in one day. Let us not put the power of the Lord to the test, as some of them did—

10 and were destroyed by serpents. Do not grumble against God, as some of them did—and were destroyed by the Destroyer.

11 All these things that happened to them were symbolic, and were recorded for our benefit as a warning. For

12 upon us the fulfilment of the ages has come. If you feel sure that you are standing firm, beware! You may fall.

13 So far you have faced no trial beyond what man can bear. God keeps faith, and he will not allow you to be tested above your powers, but when the test comes he will at the same time provide a way out, by enabling you to sustain it.

* The motive for the strict self-discipline to which Paul subjects himself is the fear that 'after preaching to others' he should find himself 'rejected', judged by God to be unfit for the final glorious destiny which he promises to others. This reminds him once more of the complacency and self-satisfaction of many of his converts, whose attitude is quite the opposite of his own. Using as an example the past history of the Israelites (God's chosen people in previous centuries), he warns his readers that their eventual salvation is not automatically secured by their becoming members of the Church (God's chosen people at the present time).

1–5. It looks as though the Corinthians expected salvation to be automatically guaranteed to them because they had been baptized and because they shared in the Lord's Supper. There were pagan religious cults which offered an automatic and almost magical salvation as a result of participation in similar ceremonies. Paul points out that the Israelites in the desert had received a kind of baptism. Just as the Christian convert was immersed in water and emerged rescued from the domination of sin, so the Israelites had travelled through the midst of the Red Sea, with the waters on either side, and had reached safety on the opposite shore, freed from the evil tyranny of the Pharaoh of Egypt (Exod. 14: 15–31). And just as Christian baptism was the ceremony of entrance into the community which owes allegiance to Christ, so the Israelites were baptized *into the fellowship of Moses*. The experience of the Exodus from Egypt made them into a community owing loyalty to Moses as its leader. (The *pillar of cloud* is mentioned in Exod. 13: 21–2 as a sign of the protecting presence of God with his people. It is not really clear why Paul should regard it as a symbol of baptism.)

The Israelites also had a form of Lord's Supper. The equivalent of the bread was the *supernatural food* God provided for them in the form of manna (Exod. 16). The equivalent of the wine was the *supernatural drink* produced when Moses caused water to spring from the rock in Horeb by striking it with his rod (Exod. 17: 6). There is no reference in the Old Testament itself to the belief that this rock was a *supernatural rock that accompanied their travels*. There was, however, a later Jewish legend that the well of water produced by the action of Moses mysteriously travelled with the Israelites, providing them with continual refreshment. Paul adds: *and that rock was Christ*. As we have discovered already (8: 6), he believed that Christ shared the functions of God himself, and had done so from the very beginning. Just as Christ was active in the creation of the world, so he shared in God's protective care of his people

73

during their wanderings in the desert. To sum up, the Israelites had possessed and made use of sacramental rites of their own. *And yet, most of them were not accepted by God, for the desert was strewn with their corpses.* They had fallen into sin and had been duly punished for it. The same thing, it is implied, may happen to Christians.

6–10. We now have a list of five examples of the Israelites' wrongdoing, as a warning to Christians to avoid sins of a similar kind.

(i) They *set* their *desires on evil things*; an allusion to the story in Num. 11: 4–6, where the people long for the food they used to eat in Egypt.

(ii) They committed idolatry: '*the people sat down to feast and stood up to play*'; a quotation of Exod. 32: 6, which describes the feasting and dancing which followed the sacrifices made to the golden calf.

(iii) They committed fornication. This story is found in Num. 25: 1–9, where the Israelites have intercourse with the Moabite women.

(iv) They *put the power of the Lord to the test*. The reference to being *destroyed by serpents* shows that this is an allusion to Num. 21: 4–9. The Israelites indicate their distrust of God, their inclination to test his powers rather than simply having faith that he can provide for them, by complaining that they have been led out of Egypt only to die in the desert.

(v) They grumbled against God. This refers to the revolt against Moses led by Korah, Dathan and Abiram (Num. 16).

11. All these events have something to do with the lives of Christians, many centuries later, since it is upon Christians that *the fulfilment of the ages has come*. Paul and his contemporaries firmly believed that in their generation, beginning with the life of Jesus, all the Old Testament prophecies were being fulfilled. This idea is extended to include the thought that the events narrated in the historical books of the Old Testament may have parallels in the life of the Church. ✻

74

THE PROBLEM OF IDOL MEAT AGAIN

So then, dear friends, shun idolatry. I speak to you as 14, 15
men of sense. Form your own judgement on what I say.
When we bless 'the cup of blessing', is it not a means of 16
sharing in the blood of Christ? When we break the bread,
is it not a means of sharing in the body of Christ? Because 17
there is one loaf, we, many as we are, are one body; for
it is one loaf of which we all partake.

Look at the Jewish people. Are not those who partake 18
in the sacrificial meal sharers in the altar? What do I 19
imply by this? that an idol is anything but an idol? or
food offered to it anything more than food? No: but the 20
sacrifices the heathen offer are offered (in the words of
Scripture) 'to demons and to that which is not God';
and I will not have you become partners with demons.
You cannot drink the cup of the Lord and the cup of 21
demons. You cannot partake of the Lord's table and the
table of demons. Can we defy the Lord? Are we stronger 22
than he?

'We are free to do anything', you say. Yes, but is 23
everything good for us? 'We are free to do anything', but
does everything help the building of the community?
Each of you must regard, not his own interests, but the 24
other man's.

You may eat anything sold in the meat-market without 25
raising questions of conscience; for the earth is the Lord's 26
and everything in it.

If an unbeliever invites you to a meal and you care 27
to go, eat whatever is put before you, without raising
questions of conscience. But if somebody says to you, 28

'This food has been offered in sacrifice', then, out of
consideration for him, and for conscience' sake, do not
29 eat it—not your conscience, I mean, but the other man's.

'What?' you say, 'is my freedom to be called in
30 question by another man's conscience? If I partake with
thankfulness, why am I blamed for eating food over which
31 I have said grace?' Well, whether you eat or drink, or
whatever you are doing, do all for the honour of God:
32 give no offence to Jews, or Greeks, or to the church of
33 God. For my part I always try to meet everyone half-
way, regarding not my own good but the good of the
11 many, so that they may be saved. Follow my example
as I follow Christ's.

✳ The problem of sacrificial meat may have been recalled to
Paul's mind by the preceding reference to the sin of idolatry.
See pp. 3-4 for a discussion of the question whether Paul here
contradicts what he has previously said in chapter 8. It was
suggested there that after writing chapter 8 he may have
come to realize that, for a Christian, there were more powerful objections to 'sitting down to a meal in a heathen temple'
than the considerations he had already mentioned.

14-22. The main objection is that it puts a Christian in
dangerous contact with *demons*. It is true that idols have no
real existence. They are not divine beings to whom worship
is due. Nevertheless, they are used by evil spiritual powers
in order to prevent men and women from worshipping the
true God. To prove that sacrificial feasts really are a means of
communicating with unseen spiritual beings, Paul refers to the
religious practices of *the Jewish people. Are not those who partake
in the sacrificial meal sharers in the altar?* The term 'altar', in
Jewish fashion, is a reverent way of speaking of God himself.
Priests, Levites and ordinary worshippers are brought into
contact with God through the eating of the sacrificed animals.

The origin of this belief is possibly the idea that, since part of the animal is offered to God, God and his worshippers are sharing a common meal, and this, according to oriental ways of thought, creates a bond of fellowship between them. A further objection is that to join in pagan sacrificial meals destroys the Christian's contact with Christ. *You cannot drink the cup of the Lord and the cup of demons. You cannot partake of the Lord's table and the table of demons.* Christians have their own sacrificial feast, the Lord's Supper, and for them this is a means of encountering Christ himself. The drinking of '*the cup of blessing*', a cup of wine representing the one which Jesus had blessed at the Last Supper, is *a means of sharing in the blood of Christ*, and the breaking and eating of the bread is *a means of sharing in the body of Christ*. Jesus is invisibly present, and through the symbolic actions of his human representatives he makes available to each individual Christian the spiritual benefits which he secured in principle for the whole human race as a result of his death. Therefore, to join in the Lord's Supper and at the same time to continue to indulge in practices which put one in touch with evil spirits who are hostile to Christ is simply an act of defiance directed against Christ himself. And since, as Paul puts it, we are not *stronger than he*, we shall be the worse for it.

23–33. This is for the most part a repetition of what has been said or implied in chapter 8. ✳

THE SUBORDINATE POSITION OF WOMEN

I commend you for always keeping me in mind, and ₂ maintaining the tradition I handed on to you. But I wish ₃ you to understand that, while every man has Christ for his Head, woman's head is man, as Christ's Head is God. A man who keeps his head covered when he prays or pro- ₄ phesies brings shame on his head; a woman, on the con- ₅ trary, brings shame on her head if she prays or prophesies

bare-headed: it is as bad as if her head were shaved.
6 If a woman is not to wear a veil she might as well have
her hair cut off; but if it is a disgrace for her to be cropped
7 and shaved, then she should wear a veil. A man has no
need to cover his head, because man is the image of God,
and the mirror of his glory, whereas woman reflects the
8 glory of man. For man did not originally spring from
9 woman, but woman was made out of man; and man was
not created for woman's sake, but woman for the sake of
10 man; and therefore it is woman's duty to have a sign of
11 authority on her head, out of regard for the angels. And
yet, in Christ's fellowship woman is as essential to man as
12 man to woman. If woman was made out of man, it is
through woman that man now comes to be; and God
is the source of all.

13   Judge for yourselves: is it fitting for a woman to pray
14 to God bare-headed? Does not Nature herself teach you
15 that while flowing locks disgrace a man, they are a
woman's glory? For her locks were given for covering.
16   However, if you insist on arguing, let me tell you,
there is no such custom among us, or in any of the
congregations of God's people.

✳ Next, Paul turns his attention to various problems of public
worship. First, he has to deal with the conduct of certain
women members of the congregation who were taking an
active part in the church service without wearing veils over
their faces. This seems to us a very trivial matter. To Paul it
was important because it symbolized an attitude of mind to
which he objected. When the Corinthian women discarded
their veils this was a conscious attempt to assert their equality
with the men in the congregation. Paul argues that, on the
contrary, women are by nature subordinate to men. In their

dress they should therefore indicate that they are subject to masculine authority. He also maintains that it is the natural and decent thing for women to have their heads covered.

3. Here we have the basic theological principle upon which Paul's practical instructions are based. It is a kind of diagram of divine–human relationships, a graded scale of authority showing who must be obedient to whom: *every man has Christ for his Head, woman's head is man, as Christ's Head is God.* If we draw the diagram it looks like this:

God
|
Christ
|
Man
|
Woman

The obedience of Christ the Son to God the Father is emphasized particularly in the Fourth Gospel, and is also mentioned in the present letter where the writer is referring to the work of Christ after his resurrection (15: 24–8). Paul's belief that all men, not only the members of the Church, ought to obey Christ, derives from his conviction that Christ himself had something to do with the creation of mankind (8: 6). If men were brought into existence by him it is self-evident that they exist for his sake, to do what he wishes. The reason why women should obey men is explained in verses 7–9.

7–9. These verses continue the theological argument, so it will be convenient to comment on them at this point and then to return to the practical issue dealt with in verses 4–6. The relative inferiority of women is part of the created order of things: *man is the image of God, and the mirror of his glory, whereas woman reflects the glory of man.* Because man is made in God's image he is like God in character, and one of the ways in which he resembles God is that he is able to exercise authority. God rules over the whole created universe, but he has delegated some of his authority to men, so that they may control the earth which they inhabit. It is implied that men are created in God's image but that women are not, and, consequently, that men possess this delegated authority but that women do not possess it. It therefore follows that men are superior to women and that women should obey them. By doing so they demonstrate the *glory of man*. They show that man holds a position of honour. The argument in these verses derives from Paul's reading of the creation stories in the first two chapters of Genesis. From the first narrative he obtains the idea that man was created in the image of God (Gen. 1: 26–7). This story does not, however, support his implied assertion that it is only men, not women, who were made in God's image. The proposal 'Let us make man in our image' refers to mankind as a whole, as the following verse shows: 'in the image of God created he him; male and female created he them'. The theme of women's natural inferiority comes from the story of Adam and Eve in Gen. 2, where God forms Eve from a rib of Adam's body and she is created in order to be Adam's companion and assistant: *man did not originally spring from woman, but woman was made out of man; and man was not created for woman's sake, but woman for the sake of man.*

4–5, 10. The practical conclusion to be drawn from these theological considerations is that women should acknowledge their divinely appointed status by wearing veils as *a sign of authority*. Veils are a sign that they regard themselves as subordinate to the authority of men. This is to be done *out of regard for the angels*. Here the angels are thought of as the guardians of the world God has created, concerned to see that his laws are obeyed, and offended, therefore, by any action which disregards them. If a woman without a veil should lead the congregation in prayer, or if she should deliver some prophetic message, thought of as inspired by the Holy Spirit and coming direct from Christ, and should do this *bare-headed*, then she *brings shame on her head*. In this phrase, *head* is to be understood in the metaphorical sense. Women who do this show disrespect for men, who are their 'heads', that is, their superiors. A man, on the other hand, performing a similar function ought not to cover his head: *A man who keeps his head covered when he prays or prophesies brings shame on his head.* Again this is metaphorical. By covering his head, and so suggesting some inferiority in his position, a man shows disrespect for his own headship, his own divinely ordained possession of authority.

6, 13–15. In support of his theological argument Paul suggests two further considerations which may help to persuade his correspondents that he is right in insisting that women should be veiled. First, he claims that an unveiled woman is the same as a woman with her hair cut short (why he thinks they are the same is not really apparent). This was a disgrace for Greek women, and it was considered especially disgraceful if they cut their hair off in order to imitate men. Secondly, he says that since women by nature have long hair it is obvious that they are intended to have their heads covered —and so should complete Nature's handiwork by wearing veils. *

BEHAVIOUR AT THE LORD'S SUPPER

In giving you these injunctions I must mention a practice 17 which I cannot commend: your meetings tend to do more harm than good. To begin with, I am told that 18 when you meet as a congregation you fall into sharply divided groups; and I believe there is some truth in it (for 19 dissensions are necessary if only to show which of your members are sound). The result is that when you meet 20 as a congregation, it is impossible for you to eat the Lord's Supper, because each of you is in such a hurry to eat his 21 own, and while one goes hungry another has too much to drink. Have you no homes of your own to eat and 22 drink in? Or are you so contemptuous of the church of God that you shame its poorer members? What am I to say? Can I commend you? On this point, certainly not!

23 For the tradition which I handed on to you came to me from the Lord himself: that the Lord Jesus, on the night

24 of his arrest, took bread and, after giving thanks to God, broke it and said: 'This is my body, which is for you;

25 do this as a memorial of me.' In the same way, he took the cup after supper, and said: 'This cup is the new covenant sealed by my blood. Whenever you drink it, do this as a

26 memorial of me.' For every time you eat this bread and drink the cup, you proclaim the death of the Lord, until he comes.

27 It follows that anyone who eats the bread or drinks the cup of the Lord unworthily will be guilty of desecrating

28 the body and blood of the Lord. A man must test himself before eating his share of the bread and drinking from

29 the cup. For he who eats and drinks eats and drinks judgement on himself if he does not discern the Body.

30 That is why many of you are feeble and sick, and a

31 number have died. But if we examined ourselves, we

32 should not thus fall under judgement. When, however, we do fall under the Lord's judgement, he is disciplining us, to save us from being condemned with the rest of the world.

33 Therefore, my brothers, when you meet for a meal,

34 wait for one another. If you are hungry, eat at home, so that in meeting together you may not fall under judgement. The other matters I will arrange when I come.

✶ The conduct of the Corinthians when they meet for the *Lord's Supper* is a mockery of its true meaning. As we read this section we need to realize that what we now think of as the service of Holy Communion took place then in the course of an ordinary meal. The word 'ordinary', however, is not very appropriate, since in the oriental world eating a meal with other people was a real sign of friendship and fellowship. This was the meaning of the Christian communal meal.

18. The first thing wrong is that the congregation *fall into sharply divided groups*. This may have something to do with the party factions described in chapter 1. On the other hand, in view of the remark in verse 22 (*Or are you so contemptuous of the church of God that you shame its poorer members?*), it may have been social distinctions that were causing the trouble. Possibly the richer members were attempting to keep themselves to themselves instead of associating with the poorer Christians. In any case, divisions of this kind are a complete denial of the meaning of the meal.

20–1. Secondly, the richer Christians, who provided most of the food and drink for the meal, probably arrived at the meeting earlier than the others. The poorer members would have to work longer hours at their trades, or they might well be slaves, who were even less able to dispose of their own time. Instead of waiting for the others, the rich were in a hurry to begin, and did so. Consequently, when the poorer members arrived they would have to go hungry. Again this was a denial of Christian fellowship. Thirdly, some people actually had *too much to drink* and became intoxicated. In these circumstances it was impossible for them *to eat the Lord's Supper*. Even if they were performing the right actions and saying the correct words over the bread and the wine, they were not really concerned with what Christ meant by his words and actions at the Last Supper. They were concerned only with the satisfaction of their own appetites.

23–6. To show them how serious their ill-conduct is, Paul reminds them of what *Jesus* had said and done and what he meant by commanding that the rite should be regularly repeated. It is worth noticing that this is the earliest written record we possess of what happened at the Last Supper. The account in Mark, the earliest of the four Gospels, was written some ten years or so after the composition of the present letter. The basic point is that both at the original Last Supper and also at every Lord's Supper held by Jesus' followers the bread and the wine in some way represent *the body and blood of the Lord* (verse 27). The breaking of the bread and the pouring out of the wine symbolize Jesus himself, accepting death (the destruction of his physical body and the consequent bloodshed) as a means of establishing a *new covenant*, a new personal relationship between God and man. Every Lord's Supper is a fresh dramatization of the crucifixion. And the eating of the bread and the drinking of the wine by each of the participants is a symbol that the crucifixion vitally affects their own individual lives. These actions are more than a dramatic symbol, however. Paul's previous remarks in chapter 10 (10: 16–17) suggest that they are to be thought of as the actual means by which the results of the death of Christ become real and effective in the lives of his followers. They are the means by which each Christian is able to experience for himself the new relationship with God which the crucifixion made possible. The idea that a symbolic action not only represents in dramatic form some present or future event but also makes the event take place derives from Hebrew ways of thinking which we find illustrated in the Old Testament. The actions performed by the prophets helped to make their prophecies come true. When Jeremiah made a yoke and wore it on his neck, this was not only a sign that the kingdom of Judah would be taken over by the Babylonians, it was also an action which helped to bring about the Babylonian dominion (Jer. 27: 1–7). Such a symbol expresses, here and now, the reality of something which actually takes place at a different moment.

27–9. Since this is the meaning of the Lord's Supper, it follows that to treat the bread and the wine merely as means of appeasing hunger and thirst is an act of desecration. Materials which represent the action of the Son of God, and which are therefore holy, are being regarded as common, everyday things which a person may treat as he chooses. The

Corinthians must realize what it is that they are doing, and must test their own attitude of mind. *For he who eats and drinks eats and drinks judgement on himself if he does not discern the Body.* This may simply mean, if he does not realize that the bread he eats represents the body of Christ. But there may be a further reference to the idea of the Christian community as the Body of Christ. This theme is to be developed in the following chapter. The image signifies, among other things, that the community is united (12: 12, 13, 25, 26). This sense of unity is created and expressed at the Lord's Supper. 'Because there is one loaf, we, many as we are, are one body; for it is one loaf of which we all partake' (10: 17). By splitting up into *sharply divided groups* (verse 18) the Corinthians were denying the meaning of the rite and destroying what should have been the essential and distinguishing characteristic of their community. They had therefore become wilfully blind to the fact that as Christians they were members of Christ's Body. ✳

Spiritual Gifts

ABOUT GIFTS of the Spirit, there are some things of **12** which I do not wish you to remain ignorant.

You know how, in the days when you were still 2 pagan, you were swept off to those dumb heathen gods, however you happened to be led. For this reason I must 3 impress upon you that no one who says 'A curse on Jesus!' can be speaking under the influence of the Spirit of God. And no one can say 'Jesus is Lord!' except under the influence of the Holy Spirit.

There are varieties of gifts, but the same Spirit. There 4, 5 are varieties of service, but the same Lord. There are 6

many forms of work, but all of them, in all men, are the
7 work of the same God. In each of us the Spirit is mani-
fested in one particular way, for some useful purpose.
8 One man, through the Spirit, has the gift of wise speech,
while another, by the power of the same Spirit, can put
9 the deepest knowledge into words. Another, by the same
Spirit, is granted faith; another, by the one Spirit, gifts of
10 healing, and another miraculous powers; another has the
gift of prophecy, and another ability to distinguish true
spirits from false; yet another has the gift of ecstatic
utterance of different kinds, and another the ability to
11 interpret it. But all these gifts are the work of one and
the same Spirit, distributing them separately to each
individual at will.

* When a man became a Christian he began to be inspired and
motivated by some new inward power which was not human
in origin but came from God. This was the Holy Spirit, God
himself working through the human personality and enabling
men and women to do things which previously they would
have been incapable of doing. For the individual Christian,
the result of the activity of the Spirit of God was that he
developed some one particular *gift*, such as the power of
prophecy or the power of *healing*, which was to be used for
the benefit of the Christian community as a whole. From the
way Paul begins his discussion it appears likely that his converts had consulted him about these spiritual gifts and various
problems to which they had given rise. In the present chapter
the following difficulties are considered.

(i) Some members of the church, when apparently in a state
of supernatural inspiration, were accustomed to utter blas-
phemous cries such as '*A curse on Jesus!*'.

(ii) The possession of different spiritual gifts led to pride
and rivalry. Those who had spectacular gifts which were

obviously supernatural in origin, such as the power of miraculous healing, tended to despise those whose gifts were less striking. They doubted whether these humbler gifts were really the result of inspiration by the Spirit of God and really necessary to the life of the Church.

(iii) Those who possessed the less spectacular gifts were discouraged by the attitude of the others and were themselves beginning to wonder whether they had any useful contribution to make to the community.

(iv) Some were not content with their own gift but coveted all the other gifts as well.

2-3. Blasphemy while in a state of apparent inspiration is treated by Paul as a throw-back to his converts' pagan days. The *heathen gods* were thought to induce a condition of ecstasy in their devotees. Although Paul would regard this not as divine inspiration but as possession by an evil spirit, he did not doubt that such a state of ecstasy could occur. Whatever explanation we ourselves might give, it is clear that something was happening at Corinth which he could interpret in this way. But if a person in this abnormal condition was accustomed to curse Christ, how could anyone else in the congregation suppose him to be inspired by the Holy Spirit? The only possible answer seems to be that in some pagan religions the devotee undergoing divine inspiration would try to resist the invading power of the god and so would curse the deity by whom he felt himself being possessed. Presumably the Corinthians thought the same thing was happening when their fellow-Christians cursed Jesus.

4-11. This is a partial answer to the second problem. All forms of *work* and *service* in the Church, resulting from the *varieties of gifts* of the different members, are without exception *the work of one and the same Spirit*, the humbler forms of service no less than the more impressive functions. In chapter 14 there is a fuller discussion of some of the gifts mentioned here.

9. The gift of *faith* cannot refer to the basic belief in Christ

which is essential to all Christians, since here it is a gift be-
longing to some members of the Church and not to others.
It must mean an especially intense degree of faith, such as
Jesus describes in Mark 11: 22–4. ✶

THE BODY OF CHRIST

12 For Christ is like a single body with its many limbs and
organs, which, many as they are, together make up one
13 body. For indeed we were all brought into one body by
baptism, in the one Spirit, whether we are Jews or Greeks,
whether slaves or free men, and that one Holy Spirit was
poured out for all of us to drink.

14, 15 A body is not one single organ, but many. Suppose the
foot should say, 'Because I am not a hand, I do not belong
to the body', it does belong to the body none the less.
16 Suppose the ear were to say, 'Because I am not an eye,
I do not belong to the body', it does still belong to the
17 body. If the body were all eye, how could it hear? If
18 the body were all ear, how could it smell? But, in fact,
God appointed each limb and organ to its own place in
19 the body, as he chose. If the whole were one single organ,
20 there would not be a body at all; in fact, however, there
21 are many different organs, but one body. The eye cannot
say to the hand, 'I do not need you'; nor the head to the
22 feet, 'I do not need you.' Quite the contrary: those organs
of the body which seem to be more frail than others are
23 indispensable, and those parts of the body which we
regard as less honourable are treated with special honour.
To our unseemly parts is given a more than ordinary
24 seemliness, whereas our seemly parts need no adorning.
But God has combined the various parts of the body,

giving special honour to the humbler parts, so that there 25
might be no sense of division in the body, but that all
its organs might feel the same concern for one another.
If one organ suffers, they all suffer together. If one 26
flourishes, they all rejoice together.

Now you are Christ's body, and each of you a limb or 27
organ of it. Within our community God has appointed, 28
in the first place apostles, in the second place prophets,
thirdly teachers; then miracle-workers, then those who
have gifts of healing, or ability to help others or power
to guide them, or the gift of ecstatic utterance of various
kinds. Are all apostles? all prophets? all teachers? Do 29
all work miracles? Have all gifts of healing? Do all 30
speak in tongues of ecstasy? Can all interpret them? The 31
higher gifts are those you should aim at.

And now I will show you the best way of all.

✶ By way of completing his answer to the problems we have
mentioned Paul develops his idea of the Church as the Body
of Christ. His converts from paganism might have been
already acquainted with the notion that a community of
people resembles a body, an organism of which each separate
part has a definite function to perform. The idea is found in
the doctrines of Stoicism, which was probably the most
popular type of philosophy in the Mediterranean world in the
time of Paul. The Stoics thought of the whole world as a
single community or, in political terms, a single state, and
they described this community as a body of which each
human being was a limb. One of these philosophers, Epictetus,
says to a pupil: 'You are a citizen of the world and one of
its limbs.' But Paul's doctrine of the Church has rather
more to it. The Church is not only similar to a body (any
body that one cares to think of). It is *Christ's body*, the body of
a particular person. This idea partly derives from the Jewish

habit of thinking of a group of people, such as a family, as constituting a single personality (see 7: 14). Christ and his followers are one person. Just as the members of Achan's family were involved in the results of his action as though they had themselves been responsible for it (Josh. 7), so Christ's followers are intimately involved in and identified with the actions of Christ. Nevertheless, there is a difference between Achan and his family on the one hand and Christ and his Church on the other. Achan would have been affected by the actions of the other members of his family in the same way that they were affected by what he had done. In his case it was a two-way process. But Christ is not affected by the actions of his followers. It is his actions that become theirs; their actions do not become his. The Church exists only as an extension and an expression of the personality of Christ.

13. We become members of the *one body*, part of Christ's inclusive personality, *by baptism* which signifies that from this point onwards we belong to Christ (see 1: 13–17), and as a result of the work of the *Holy Spirit*, the power of God active within us to produce in our own personalities some resemblance to the character of Christ himself.

14–26. Here the doctrine of the Church as the Body of Christ is used to explain the relationship of Christians to each other, a relationship similar to that of the different *limbs* of a *single body*.

The following points emerge.

14–16. Every Christian is a necessary member of the community.

17–22. Every Christian needs the help of every other Christian.

23–5. Particular respect should be shown to those members of the community who appear to be less important than the rest.

25–6. Every Christian is sympathetically involved in the prosperity or misfortune of his fellow-Christians.

There is therefore no reason for the more distinguished members of the congregation to despise the humbler members or to ignore them, nor for the apparently less important ones to feel that they have no proper place in the life of the community.

27–31. Since the gifts of the Spirit have been distributed by God, and since no one gift is possessed by every member of the Church nor does any one member possess them all, there is no cause for coveting gifts one has not received. On the other hand it is allowable to *aim at* acquiring the *higher gifts*. ✳

THE SUPREMACY OF LOVE

I may speak in tongues of men or of angels, but if I am **13** without love, I am a sounding gong or a clanging cymbal. I may have the gift of prophecy, and know every hidden 2 truth; I may have faith strong enough to move mountains; but if I have no love, I am nothing. I may dole out 3 all I possess, or even give my body to be burnt, but if I have no love, I am none the better.

Love is patient; love is kind and envies no one. Love 4 is never boastful, nor conceited, nor rude; never selfish, 5 not quick to take offence. Love keeps no score of wrongs; does not gloat over other men's sins, but delights in the 6 truth. There is nothing love cannot face; there is no 7 limit to its faith, its hope, and its endurance.

Love will never come to an end. Are there prophets? 8 their work will be over. Are there tongues of ecstasy? they will cease. Is there knowledge? it will vanish away; for our knowledge and our prophecy alike are partial, 9 and the partial vanishes when wholeness comes. When 10,11 I was a child, my speech, my outlook, and my thoughts were all childish. When I grew up, I had finished with childish things. Now we see only puzzling reflections 12

in a mirror, but then we shall see face to face. My
knowledge now is partial; then it will be whole, like

13 God's knowledge of me. In a word, there are three
things that last for ever: faith, hope, and love; but the
greatest of them all is love.

✻ The discussion of spiritual gifts is taken up again in chapter
14. The present chapter is a slight digression from the main
argument, but not entirely unconnected with it. *Love* is
different from the gifts Paul has been speaking of because it is
a quality which must belong to all Christians, not only to
particular members of the community. It is like those gifts,
however, in so far as love in the Christian sense is just as much
the result of the supernatural power of the Holy Spirit as are
any of the particular gifts (Gal. 5: 22). Also it is the quality
which enables each Christian to behave as a member of the
Body of Christ, showing consideration and respect for the
other members. The theme of chapter 13 is that love is more
important than any of the other spiritual gifts, that without
love they are valueless, and that love is permanent whereas
they are of use only in the period of time preceding the
coming of Christ and the final judgement.

1. The gift of speaking *in tongues of men or of angels* refers
to the inspired outpouring of ecstatic but unintelligible speech
which will be further discussed in the following chapter. The
mention of angels suggests that the speech was sometimes so
sublime that it seemed to be entirely different from any kind
of human language, and so exalted in character that it re-
sembled human ideas of what angelic speech was like. The
point of the comparison with *a sounding gong or a clanging
cymbal* is that these instruments produce noise but no melody,
and therefore have no musical value in themselves. In the same
way, a person gifted with ecstatic utterance but lacking in
love may produce an impressive (and perhaps noisy) display of
religious emotion, but this will have no genuine value, either
for the person himself or for the congregation as a whole.

2. Compare Mark 11: 22–4.

3. For the idea of distributing one's possessions compare Acts 4: 34–7, which describes how the wealthier members of the Jerusalem church (among them Paul's colleague Barnabas) sold their property, whether houses or lands, so that the money could be used to help their needy fellow-Christians. The exact meaning of the second form of self-sacrifice (*or even give my body to be burnt*) is not so clear. It may refer to a Christian who voluntarily seeks martyrdom, the form of execution being death by burning. This had happened to some of the faithful Jews during the persecution instigated by Antiochus Epiphanes (2 Macc. 7). It is true that burning was not a form of punishment generally practised by Romans or Greeks, and some scholars have therefore rejected this interpretation on the grounds that being burnt alive was not an actual danger, or even a hypothetical possibility, to Paul or to his converts. Nevertheless, we are told by the Roman historian Tacitus that the Emperor Nero, some ten years or so after the writing of the present letter, caused numbers of Christians to suffer death by burning after they had been arrested on suspicion of having been responsible for the great fire at Rome. It was not therefore a completely unknown form of torture. Alternatively, the reference to burning may be an allusion to the custom of branding slaves as a mark of ownership. The idea would then be that some Christians might even sell themselves as slaves in order to get money to give to the poor. We have to choose, then, between voluntary martyrdom or voluntary slavery. A decision is difficult. Selling oneself as a slave might follow naturally upon the idea of selling one's possessions for the benefit of the poor. On the other hand, if the phrase is meant to suggest the supreme example of Christian heroism, martyrdom fits the context better.

7. The terms *faith* and *hope* do not refer to one's relationship with God but to one's attitude to one's neighbour. The person who possesses love believes the best about other people,

and even if his neighbour has obviously done something wrong he continues to hope that his conduct will improve.

8-11. The rather vague term *wholeness* must mean the life which follows the resurrection of the dead, the final state of blessedness and glory into which all believers will eventually be transformed. *Love will never come to an end*, neither in this life nor in the life of the resurrection, because it is the basis of the permanent relationship between God and man which lasts for all eternity. On the other hand, if we consider *prophecy*, *tongues of ecstasy*, and whatever *knowledge* of God may be communicated to the members of the Church here and now, it is plain that all these things are only means whereby contact takes place between God and man during our present earthly life. They will eventually cease to be of use, just as an adult person has no more use for the *speech*, *outlook*, and *thought* of his childhood.

12. The explanation is that gifts such as prophecy give us only an indirect, second-hand, fragmentary knowledge of God. In the life of the world to come we shall see him *face to face*. Our knowledge of him will be first-hand, complete.

13. This verse presents a difficulty. Certainly the main point is that *love* is the most important gift or quality of all. The problem is what Paul means when he says *there are three things that last for ever: faith, hope, and love*. Had he spoken of *love* only, then he would simply be repeating what he has already said in verse 8. The words *for ever* could be taken in their literal sense. But can *faith* and *hope* be said literally to last *for ever*? Elsewhere in his letters he treats them as qualities which belong only to the present life. In 2 Cor. 5: 7 believing in Christ during one's earthly existence is contrasted with actually seeing him in the life to come. In Rom. 8: 23-5 hope is our proper attitude 'while we wait for God to . . . set our whole body free', i.e. while we wait for the resurrection (after which event there will be no more necessity for hope). It may be, therefore, that the verse is to be interpreted in the sense that *faith, hope, and love* are permanently characteristic of the

Christian during his whole earthly life. On the other hand, since the future life has just been mentioned in the preceding verses, it is much more natural to take *last for ever* as an allusion to it. In that case we should have to understand *faith* and *hope* as a general attitude of complete dependence and reliance upon God, an attitude as necessary in the life of the resurrection as it is now. ✳

A COMPARISON OF GIFTS

Put love first; but there are other gifts of the Spirit at **14** which you should aim also, and above all prophecy. When a man is using the language of ecstasy he is talking 2 with God, not with men, for no man understands him; he is no doubt inspired, but he speaks mysteries. On the 3 other hand, when a man prophesies, he is talking to men, and his words have power to build; they stimulate and they encourage. The language of ecstasy is good for the 4 speaker himself, but it is prophecy that builds up a Christian community. I should be pleased for you all to 5 use the tongues of ecstasy, but better pleased for you to prophesy. The prophet is worth more than the man of ecstatic speech—unless indeed he can explain its meaning, and so help to build up the community. Suppose, my 6 friends, that when I come to you I use ecstatic language: what good shall I do you, unless what I say contains something by way of revelation, or enlightenment, or prophecy, or instruction?

Even with inanimate things that produce sounds—a 7 flute, say, or a lyre—unless their notes mark definite intervals, how can you tell what tune is being played? Or again, if the trumpet-call is not clear, who will pre- 8

9 pare for battle? In the same way if your ecstatic utterance yields no precise meaning, how can anyone tell what you
10 are saying? You will be talking into the air. How many different kinds of sound there are, or may be, in the
11 world! Nothing is altogether soundless. Well then, if I do not know the meaning of the sound the speaker makes,
12 his words will be gibberish to me, and mine to him. You are, I know, eager for gifts of the Spirit; then aspire above all to excel in those which build up the church.

13   I say, then, that the man who falls into ecstatic utterance
14 should pray for the ability to interpret. If I use such language in my prayer, the Spirit in me prays, but my
15 intellect lies fallow. What then? I will pray as I am inspired to pray, but I will also pray intelligently. I will sing hymns as I am inspired to sing, but I will sing in-
16 telligently too. Suppose you are praising God in the language of inspiration: how will the plain man who is present be able to say 'Amen' to your thanksgiving, when
17 he does not know what you are saying? Your prayer of thanksgiving may be all that could be desired, but it is no
18 help to the other man. Thank God, I am more gifted in
19 ecstatic utterance than any of you, but in the congrega- tion I would rather speak five intelligible words, for the benefit of others as well as myself, than thousands of words in the language of ecstasy.

20   Do not be childish, my friends. Be as innocent of evil
21 as babes, but at least be grown-up in your thinking. We read in the Law: 'I will speak to this nation through men of strange tongues, and by the lips of foreigners; and even
22 so they will not heed me, says the Lord.' Clearly then these 'strange tongues' are not intended as a sign for

believers, but for unbelievers, whereas prophecy is designed not for unbelievers but for those who hold the
faith. So if the whole congregation is assembled and all 23
are using the 'strange tongues' of ecstasy, and some uninstructed persons or unbelievers should enter, will they
not think you are mad? But if all are uttering prophecies, 24
the visitor, when he enters, hears from everyone something that searches his conscience and brings conviction,
and the secrets of his heart are laid bare. So he will fall 25
down and worship God, crying, 'God is certainly among
you!'

✻ Paul argues that *prophecy* is a more important and useful
gift than *ecstatic utterance*.

Prophecy corresponds quite closely to our idea of preaching.
The prophet is inspired by the Holy Spirit to deliver a message
designed to encourage the other members of the congregation in their attempts to live a Christian life (verse 3). It may
also have the effect of converting some non-Christian visitor
(verses 24-5). Elsewhere in the New Testament we discover
that prophets sometimes uttered inspired predictions of the
future, as when Agabus prophesied the arrest of Paul in
Jerusalem (Acts 21: 10-11).

The gift of *ecstatic utterance*, on the other hand, is much
more unfamiliar to us. But to Paul and his correspondents it
was so familiar that it needed no explanation or description.
We have therefore only a few vague and allusive references to
provide us with a clue to the nature of the experience. From
the present chapter we can deduce the following facts. A
person *using the language of ecstasy* appears to be supernaturally
inspired (verses 2, 14-16). He utters words or sounds which
mean nothing at all to most of the congregation, although
there may be a few people present who are themselves inspired to understand him (verses 2, 26-8) and he may be able
to *interpret* his own experience afterwards (verses 5, 13). At

97

the time he is not fully conscious himself of what he is doing (verse 14). Often the experience appears to be a form of prayer (verses 2, 14, 16–17). We might conclude that it is a state of intense religious emotion which cannot be communicated in ordinary language and which therefore expresses itself in a series of apparently meaningless and inarticulate sounds. It is not too difficult to see how a few of the listeners might be able to understand what it was about. It is true in everyday life that emotion can be communicated to other people without the use of coherent words. We can easily tell whether our friends are happy or miserable, even if they do not actually explain their feelings to us. In a similar way, someone sympathetic towards the person in a state of ecstasy might understand in general terms what his feelings were, and so would be able to explain his experience to the others.

The R.V. translation, which is a more literal rendering of the Greek, suggests that there is something more to be said about the condition in question. In this version, it is described as speaking 'in a tongue' or 'with tongues'. The term 'tongue' obviously here means 'language' rather than 'physical organ of speech'. Presumably it indicates a foreign language, or at any rate a language different from the one normally used by the inspired person. The Greek word employed, *glossa*, had become a technical term for an ancient language, an obscure dialect, a rare expression, and an unintelligible language such as that attributed to the oracle at Delphi. We might therefore be tempted to suppose that the inspired person delivered a discourse in a foreign language in the same way that the apostles, according to the author of Acts, 'began to talk in other tongues' on the Day of Pentecost (Acts 2: 4–11). But the narrative in Acts suggests that the apostles' form of speech, whatever it may have been, was intelligible to the whole audience, and this contradicts Paul's description of ecstatic utterance. Consequently the account in Acts is of doubtful value for the interpretation of the situation in Corinth. Perhaps the simplest explanation is that the person who possessed this gift was accustomed to utter a few words or phrases of some foreign language, which might be recognized as, for example, Latin or Aramaic, but which did not form coherent sentences and so remained incomprehensible. Since the population of Corinth came from all parts of the known world, the members of the church there would speak a variety of languages and dialects. It may be that a person in a state of extreme religious emotion might go back to using his own original native tongue, but in a confused manner.

4. The basic reason for preferring the gift of *prophecy* to that of *ecstatic utterance* is that the unintelligible speech of ecstasy is of no help to anyone else. It is like a musical instrument which makes unrelated and meaningless sounds instead of playing a proper melody (verse 7). The *plain man* (verse 16), the ordinary member of the congregation, ought to be able to join in all that happens in public worship, if only to the extent of following the prayers and making them his own by saying '*Amen*' at the end. How can he do this if he does not understand what the prayer is about (verses 16–17)? Ecstatic speech is therefore merely a private, individual religious experience which does not *help to build up the community* (verse 5). To regard it as the gift supremely to be desired is a form of selfishness. Prophecy is the very opposite. The essential function of the prophet is to act as a channel of communication between God and the Christian congregation. Prophecy is fundamentally something which takes place for the benefit of other people.

14–15. Even from the point of view of the ecstatic person himself the experience leaves something to be desired. *If I use such language in my prayer, the Spirit in me prays, but my intellect lies fallow*. The ideal form of communion with God is not a state of emotional ecstasy in which the Christian is not consciously aware of what is happening. It is a form of prayer which may certainly be inspired yet which is at the same time a conscious and intelligent activity. It is a process which demands the use of one's mind.

20–5. *Prophecy* is more beneficial than *ecstatic utterance* if

99

we consider the possible effects of each gift upon interested non-Christians who may happen to attend the church service. Dealing first with ecstatic utterance, Paul quotes from Isa. 28: 11–12, where God threatens to speak to the unbelieving Jews '*through men of strange tongues, and by the lips of foreigners*'. In the context this is a double punishment. They will suffer foreign invasion and God will cease to make himself known to them through the prophets. The result is that they will become even more adamant in their unbelief: '*and even so they will not heed me, says the Lord.*' The connexion with the situation in Corinth lies in the mention of '*strange tongues*'. The quotation is used in order to suggest that the effect of witnessing ecstatic utterance would be to confirm non-Christians in their unbelief and to prevent their conversion. *So if the whole congregation is assembled and all are using the 'strange tongues' of ecstasy, and some uninstructed persons or unbelievers should enter, will they not think you are mad?* Prophetic utterance, on the other hand, may move a non-Christian visitor to repentance and belief in God.

22. If the paragraph as a whole is to be interpreted in this way, we shall have to paraphrase verse 22 as follows. 'Ecstatic utterance is not intended to be something which produces belief in Christianity. It is a phenomenon which leaves non-Christians in their unbelieving state. Prophecy, on the other hand, is intended not to confirm unbelievers in their unbelief but to encourage conversion to the Christian faith.' ✻

THE ORDERING OF PUBLIC WORSHIP

26 To sum up, my friends: when you meet for worship, each of you contributes a hymn, some instruction, a revelation, an ecstatic utterance, or the interpretation of such an utterance. All of these must aim at one thing:
27 to build up the church. If it is a matter of ecstatic utterance, only two should speak, or at most three, one at a

time, and someone must interpret. If there is no inter- 28
preter, the speaker had better not address the meeting at
all, but speak to himself and to God. Of the prophets, 29
two or three may speak, while the rest exercise their
judgement upon what is said. If someone else, sitting in 30
his place, receives a revelation, let the first speaker stop.
You can all prophesy, one at a time, so that the whole 31
congregation may receive instruction and encourage-
ment. It is for prophets to control prophetic inspiration, 32
for the God who inspires them is not a God of disorder 33
but of peace.

As in all congregations of God's people, women should 34
not address the meeting. They have no licence to speak,
but should keep their place as the law directs. If there is 35
something they want to know, they can ask their own
husbands at home. It is a shocking thing that a woman
should address the congregation.

Did the word of God originate with you? Or are you 36
the only people to whom it came? If anyone claims to be 37
inspired or a prophet, let him recognize that what I write
has the Lord's authority. If he does not recognize this, 38
he himself should not be recognized.

In short, my friends, be eager to prophesy; do not 39
forbid ecstatic utterance; but let all be done decently and 40
in order.

---

* 26. *Worship* in the church at Corinth was obviously a
far less formal affair than our own church services. Each
member of the congregation was entirely free to make some
individual contribution to it as and when he felt inspired to do
so. This freedom, in conjunction with the fervent religious
enthusiasm of the Corinthians, was causing some confusion.

34–5. These verses appear to contradict 11: 5, which implies that a woman inspired to prophesy may certainly address the congregation though she must wear a veil while doing so. The only possible answer to the difficulty is that here Paul is referring not to a woman's exercise of the gift of prophecy, which he did not forbid, but to the practice of women joining in the congregational discussion of what a prophet or a teacher had said. The Greek does not in fact say *women should not address the meeting* (a translation which suggests a prophetic discourse) but that women should remain silent in the assembly.

37. Paul claims to have *the Lord's authority* for what he has written. As an apostle he speaks on behalf of Christ himself. ✿

Life After Death

THE RESURRECTION OF JESUS

15 AND NOW, MY BROTHERS, I must remind you of the gospel that I preached to you; the gospel which you
2 received, on which you have taken your stand, and which is now bringing you salvation. Do you still hold fast the Gospel as I preached it to you? If not, your conversion was in vain.

3 First and foremost, I handed on to you the facts which had been imparted to me: that Christ died for our sins,
4 in accordance with the scriptures; that he was buried; that he was raised to life on the third day, according to
5 the scriptures; and that he appeared to Cephas, and after-
6 wards to the Twelve. Then he appeared to over five hundred of our brothers at once, most of whom are still

alive, though some have died. Then he appeared to 7
James, and afterwards to all the apostles.

In the end he appeared even to me; though this birth of 8
mine was monstrous, for I had persecuted the church and 9
am therefore inferior to all other apostles—indeed not fit
to be called an apostle. However, by God's grace I am 10
what I am, nor has his grace been given to me in vain;
on the contrary, in my labours I have outdone them all—
not I, indeed, but the grace of God working with me.
But what matter, I or they? This is what we all proclaim, 11
and this is what you believed.

* The chapter as a whole contains two main themes: the
assertion that the resurrection of the dead will really take place
and an attempt to describe what the resurrection life will be
like. Throughout the discussion we need to bear in mind that
Paul does not think of this as a purely spiritual existence but
as a life in which the restored human personality will possess
some kind of bodily form. A further point to notice is that
the title *Life After Death* is somewhat misleading. The resurrection life does not begin for the individual Christian immediately he dies. The resurrection of all Christians together is to
take place at the same moment, at the coming of Christ. The
reason for the introduction of the topic in the present letter is
that some Corinthians were denying that there would ever be
a resurrection of the dead. So much is clear, but their reasons
for holding this view are not so plain. It is possible that they
believed simply in the immortality of the soul, regarding the
body as a kind of tomb in which the soul was imprisoned. In
that case the future existence they would hope for after death
would not be bodily resurrection but the state described by
Plato in the *Phaedo*, 'when the soul is by itself, apart from the
body'. Perhaps they were reacting against popular Jewish
views of the resurrection which suggested that it would be
this present physical life all over again. The *Apocalypse of*

Baruch claims that the physical characteristics of the body in this life are perpetuated in the risen body in order that the dead may be recognizable when they are raised. We may compare the question put to Jesus by the Sadducees about the woman who had been married to seven husbands: whose wife would she be in the life of the resurrection (Mark 12: 18–23)? On the other hand, it is also possible that the Corinthians were inclined to deny that there was any future life after death at all, at any rate any kind of life worthy of the name. They may have been influenced by the more ancient Greek ideas of the survival of ghosts in the underworld. This was a dreary and shadowy existence, not life in the true sense of the word. These various possibilities are not mutually exclusive. It is quite likely that there were several different ideas about the future state going around among the Corinthian Christians, and that the one thing they had in common was a denial of the resurrection of the body.

The argument begins with a reminder of the basic facts of the Christian faith, chiefly the fact of the resurrection of Jesus himself, an event well-attested by a number of reliable witnesses.

3–4. Both the death and the resurrection of Christ are said to have taken place *in accordance with the scriptures*. If this refers to any specific passage in the Old Testament perhaps the most likely one is the description in Isa. 53 of the suffering and the subsequent exaltation of the Servant of the Lord. Alternatively, Paul's phrase may mean that these events happened in accordance with the fundamental significance of Scripture as a whole. This is little more than saying that Christ's death and resurrection were part of God's plan for mankind, a plan of which the earlier stages are recorded in the Old Testament.

5. The appearance *to Cephas* is referred to in Luke 24: 34, and that *to the Twelve* may be the one which follows in Luke's narrative (verses 36–49); Luke speaks of 'the Eleven' which is historically correct, since Judas had committed suicide after

his betrayal of Jesus; Paul uses 'the Twelve' as a collective term indicating Jesus' original disciples.

6. This appearance cannot be identified for certain with any of the events recorded in the Gospels.

7. *James* is the brother of Jesus; in Paul's day James was the leader of the Jerusalem church. Again, we are told nothing of this appearance in the Gospels, nor of the one *to all the apostles*, a phrase which presumably includes more than the Eleven and possibly refers to missionaries such as Barnabas.

8–9. See Acts 9: 1–19 for the story of the appearance of Christ to Paul on his way to Damascus. ✳

THE RESURRECTION OF CHRISTIANS AS A FUTURE REALITY

Now if this is what we proclaim, that Christ was raised 12 from the dead, how can some of you say there is no resurrection of the dead? If there be no resurrection, then 13 Christ was not raised; and if Christ was not raised, then 14 our gospel is null and void, and so is your faith; and we 15 turn out to be lying witnesses for God, because we bore witness that he raised Christ to life, whereas, if the dead are not raised, he did not raise him. For if the dead are 16 not raised, it follows that Christ was not raised; and if 17 Christ was not raised, your faith has nothing in it and you are still in your old state of sin. It follows also that those 18 who have died within Christ's fellowship are utterly lost. If it is for this life only that Christ has given us hope, we 19 of all men are most to be pitied.

But the truth is, Christ was raised to life—the firstfruits 20 of the harvest of the dead. For since it was a man who 21 brought death into the world, a man also brought resurrection of the dead. As in Adam all men die, so in 22

23 Christ all will be brought to life; but each in his own
proper place: Christ the firstfruits, and afterwards, at his
24 coming, those who belong to Christ. Then comes the end,
when he delivers up the kingdom to God the Father, after
abolishing every kind of domination, authority, and
25 power. For he is destined to reign until God has put all
26 enemies under his feet; and the last enemy to be abolished
27 is death. Scripture says, 'He has put all things in sub-
jection under his feet.' But in saying 'all things', it clearly
28 means to exclude God who subordinates them; and when
all things are thus subject to him, then the Son himself will
also be made subordinate to God who made all things
subject to him, and thus God will be all in all.

29   Again, there are those who receive baptism on behalf
of the dead. Why should they do this? If the dead are
not raised to life at all, what do they mean by being
baptized on their behalf?

30   And we ourselves—why do we face these dangers hour
31 by hour? Every day I die: I swear it by my pride in you,
my brothers—for in Christ Jesus our Lord I am proud of
32 you. If, as the saying is, I 'fought wild beasts' at Ephesus,
what have I gained by it? If the dead are never raised
to life, 'let us eat and drink, for tomorrow we die'.

33   Make no mistake: 'Bad company is the ruin of a good
34 character.' Come back to a sober and upright life and
leave your sinful ways. There are some who know nothing
of God; to your shame I say it.

✳ In this section Paul sets out to do three things. First, to
show the impossible and ridiculous conclusions which logically
follow from a denial that there is any *resurrection of the dead*
(verses 12–19). Secondly, to show that the resurrection of

Christ will eventually bring about the resurrection of Christians also, as its logical result (verses 20-8). Thirdly, to show that his own activity, and the activity of other Christians, is futile if the resurrection of the dead is not a future reality (verses 29-32).

13, 16. The first absurd and impossible conclusion is this. If the dead are completely incapable of being restored to life, if such a process is entirely alien to the nature of man, *then Christ was not raised*. Jesus was fully human. As a man he could not undergo any experience or any process which in principle it would be impossible for other human beings to undergo. Therefore, *if the dead are not raised*, the resurrection of Jesus cannot have occurred. But this conclusion is ridiculous. Paul has just proved (verses 4-8) that the resurrection of Jesus is an authentic historical fact. It follows that the first stage of the argument, denial of resurrection as a general possibility, is absurd as well.

17. Secondly, Paul tells his converts *your faith has nothing in it and you are still in your old state of sin*. He thinks of death as the result of man's sin, and its punishment (cf. Rom. 6: 23). Sin and Death are imagined as twin powers which control man's existence. The resurrection of Jesus meant the defeat of Death, and consequently the defeat of Sin also. But *if Christ was not raised* then Death has not been defeated and neither has Sin. In that case human existence is still under Sin's control. This, however, the Corinthians know to be untrue from their own personal experience. It is a ridiculous conclusion to arrive at. In their own daily lives they know that Sin's power over them has been broken. Therefore it is absurd to say that the resurrection of Jesus did not take place. But this, as we have seen, is the logical conclusion to which we are led if we deny that the dead can be raised. It follows that the denial itself is absurd.

18-19. Thirdly, to deny the resurrection forces us to conclude that the members of the Church who have died already *are utterly lost*. This means that our present Christian life is a pitiable affair, since the knowledge of God and the experience of his love which a Christian enjoys are impermanent and ultimately futile.

20–3. The well-attested fact of the resurrection of Jesus himself involves as its necessary consequence the resurrection of all *those who belong to Christ*. This is explained by means of a comparison and contrast between what Adam did and what the results of his action were and what Christ has done and what the results of his action will be. According to the story in Gen. 3, Adam disobeyed God and so God pronounced upon him the sentence of eventual death: 'dust thou art, and unto dust shalt thou return'. In the myth he is driven out of the Garden of Eden lest he should eat of the fruit of the tree of life and so secure immortality. This sentence of death was valid not only for Adam as an individual but also for all his descendants, for the whole human race: *in Adam all men die*. Some of the Jewish rabbis taught in a quite naïve way that all the future generations of mankind were contained within the physical body of Adam, so that they were inevitably affected by what happened to him. They also sin and they also die. Paul seems to have accepted this general idea. Both here and in Rom. 5 he uses it as an illustration to show how what had happened to Jesus as an individual inevitably affects his followers as well. *For since it was a man who brought death into the world, a man also brought resurrection of the dead*. Christ resembles Adam because what happens to him potentially affects the whole human race. He differs from Adam because Adam brought about the death of mankind, whereas *in Christ all will be brought to life* as a result of his resurrection. If Paul were to be asked for a further explanation of what he meant by saying that something happens to people 'in Christ', he would no doubt refer to the conception of the Church as the Body of Christ. Christians are included within the personality of Christ, so that his experience of resurrection will become theirs, and the imperishable immortality he now enjoys will eventually belong to them as well.

24–6. When Christ returns and the resurrection takes place, this will be *the end*, when he *delivers up the kingdom to God the Father*. That is, his work as Messiah will be completed. As Messiah he is the divinely appointed king, and his rule is in force in the period of time between his resurrection and his return. His function as ruler is to overcome and abolish *every kind of domination, authority, and power*, all the forces of evil, human or non-human, and every form of being in the whole universe which is hostile to God. *For he is destined to reign until God has put all enemies under his feet. Death* is here personified as one of these enemies, the supreme evil power. The preliminary defeat of Death took place when Jesus was raised from the dead, but complete victory will not be achieved until the general resurrection occurs. When this happens, it will show that all the forces of evil have been at last annihilated. The messianic function of Christ will therefore come to an end. He will give back to God the Father the powers entrusted to him for carrying it out, and will present to God a universe throughout which his sovereignty is perfectly established.

27. Ps. 8: 6 is applied to Christ, as scriptural evidence that God's own authority has been delegated to him.

28. This is a repetition in slightly different words of the idea expressed in verse 24. When Paul says that *the Son himself will also be made subordinate to God*, he is not attempting to describe the relationship between the Son and the Father within the eternal being of God. He is referring only to the conclusion of the work of the Son within the present created universe. The statement that *God will be all in all* means either that God's kingdom will be completely established throughout the whole universe, or possibly that God will be the sole object of contemplation and adoration by all created beings.

29. Various aspects of Christian life make no sense if there is no resurrection. Why do some people *receive baptism on behalf of the dead*? It is uncertain what this practice was. Perhaps some members of the congregation underwent further bap-

tisms on behalf of friends or relatives who had received instruction in the Christian faith but had died before they had
themselves been baptized. If there was to be no real future
existence how could they possibly benefit in any way at
all?

30–2. Why are the apostles ready to endanger their lives?
They will get nothing out of it in the end if the dead are not
raised. We must note that although it was literally true that
the apostles sometimes had to face the possibility of martyrdom, nevertheless the reference here to fighting '*wild beasts*' is
metaphorical. If Paul had ever been sentenced to fight wild
animals in the arena at Ephesus he would surely have mentioned it in 2 Cor. 11: 23–7, where he gives a list of the various
dangers he has encountered in the course of his missionary
activity. He is probably referring to the kind of mob-violence
which sometimes resulted from his preaching, often at the
instigation of the Jewish section of the population.

32*b*. A quotation of Isa. 22: 13.

33. A quotation from the play *Thais* by the Greek drama-
tist Menander. *

THE RESURRECTION LIFE

35 But, you may ask, how are the dead raised? In what kind
36 of body? A senseless question! The seed you sow does
37 not come to life unless it has first died; and what you
    sow is not the body that shall be, but a naked grain, per-
38 haps of wheat, or of some other kind; and God clothes
    it with the body of his choice, each seed with its own
39 particular body. All flesh is not the same flesh: there is
    flesh of men, flesh of beasts, of birds, and of fishes—all
40 different. There are heavenly bodies and earthly bodies;
    and the splendour of the heavenly bodies is one thing, the
41 splendour of the earthly, another. The sun has a splendour

of its own, the moon another splendour, and the stars
another, for star differs from star in brightness. So it is 42
with the resurrection of the dead. What is sown in the
earth as a perishable thing is raised imperishable. Sown in 43
humiliation, it is raised in glory; sown in weakness, it is
raised in power; sown as an animal body, it is raised as a 44
spiritual body.

If there is such a thing as an animal body, there is also
a spiritual body. It is in this sense that Scripture says, 45
'The first man, Adam, became an animate being', whereas the last Adam has become a life-giving spirit. Observe, 46
the spiritual does not come first; the animal body comes
first, and then the spiritual. The first man was made 'of 47
the dust of the earth': the second man is from heaven. The 48
man made of dust is the pattern of all men of dust, and the
heavenly man is the pattern of all the heavenly. As we 49
have worn the likeness of the man made of dust, so we
shall wear the likeness of the heavenly man.

What I mean, my brothers, is this: flesh and blood can 50
never possess the kingdom of God, and the perishable
cannot possess immortality. Listen! I will unfold a 51
mystery: we shall not all die, but we shall all be changed in 52
a flash, in the twinkling of an eye, at the last trumpet-call.
For the trumpet will sound, and the dead will rise immortal, and we shall be changed. This perishable being must 53
be clothed with the imperishable, and what is mortal
must be clothed with immortality. And when our mor- 54
tality has been clothed with immortality, then the saying
of Scripture will come true: 'Death is swallowed up;
victory is won!' 'O Death, where is your victory? O 55
Death, where is your sting?' The sting of death is sin, and 56

57 sin gains its power from the law; but, God be praised, he gives us the victory through our Lord Jesus Christ.

58   Therefore, my beloved brothers, stand firm and immovable, and work for the Lord always, work without limit, since you know that in the Lord your labour cannot be lost.

✻ Perhaps some people were prevented from believing in the resurrection by the obvious difficulty of imagining what this sort of existence would be like.

35–44. Paul's attempt to describe it begins with an illustration from nature: the sowing of a *seed* and its growth into a plant. The seed sown in the ground corresponds to our earthly life from birth to death, and the plant which grows from the seed corresponds to our resurrection existence. The illustration seems intended to suggest the following ideas.

(i) We should not necessarily expect to know in detail what the life of the resurrection will be like (the question is a *senseless* one). No one who looks at a *grain* of *wheat* or any other seed can possibly tell from its external appearance what the plant will look like when it has grown. It is God who in a miraculous way *clothes it with the body of his choice*, that is, produces its new form. In the same way we cannot possibly guess what our own new form will be. But to allow our ignorance to cause us to doubt whether this new state of being is a reality is to doubt the power of God. This, again, is foolishness. He has already brought into existence so many different varieties of created being—men, animals, *the sun*, *the moon*, *the stars*—that we cannot deny that he is capable of even more splendid acts of creation in the future (including the creation of the resurrection body).

(ii) Since the plant differs from the seed in appearance we are not to suppose, like some of the Jews, that belief in the resurrection requires us to believe in the restoration of the material body with all its previous characteristics.

(iii) The resurrection existence will be far more glorious than our present life, just as the plant is much more impressive and beautiful than the seed.

(iv) There is continuity of some kind between our present life and the life of the resurrection. The seed and the plant are the same organism at different stages of its life-history. We shall be the same people, not different personalities entirely, when we are raised from the dead.

44 *b*–49. The difference between the two forms of existence is described as the difference between an *animal body* and a *spiritual body*. What is meant by these terms? The *animal body* stands for our present physical existence. To Paul, physical life was a kind of force or power which animated the material body, and its presence or absence was what made the difference between a living person and a corpse. This physical life is not peculiar to human beings, but is shared by the animals as well. The *animal body*, therefore, is the human being considered as part of the natural world and preserved alive by the presence of this force within him. When Paul talks of a *spiritual body* as the form our future existence will take we must first of all note that the word *body* is of considerable importance. We shall not be just disembodied spirits, little more than ghosts. We shall possess some bodily form for the expression of our personalities. Secondly, the term *spiritual* implies that our personalities will be completely controlled and directed by the Holy Spirit, the Spirit of Christ, working within our own spirits so that our whole selves become perfect replicas of the character of Christ. It is the power of the Spirit of God which will continually preserve us alive in our future existence, not the force of animal life. At this point in the argument (verse 45), we have a further parallel between Adam and Christ. According to Gen. 2: 7, ' *The first man, Adam, became an animate being* '. The form of existence which he passed on to the whole human race is life as an *animal body*, the physical life which we at present experience and which is weak and perishable in character. But Christ, *the last Adam, has become*

a life-giving spirit. Through his life, death and resurrection he has brought into being a new kind of human existence, life which is wholly controlled by the Spirit of God and so is imperishable and eternal. This eternal life he will pass on to those who have become members of his Body, the Church, and so are included within his own personality and derive their life from him. The parallel between Adam and Christ is amplified in verses 47–9. The *man made of dust* is Adam, according to the story in Genesis fashioned by God out '*of the dust of the earth*', formed from the substance of the material universe, or (in our own terms) the final product of the process of evolution in the natural world. The *heavenly man* is Christ, and this *second man*, this second kind of human existence, came into being when the Son of God 'came down from heaven' and, as Jesus of Nazareth, began to live a human life. In verse 46 Paul thinks it necessary to point out that the type of human life symbolized by Adam *comes first.* In the history of the universe, it precedes in time the kind of life brought into existence by the birth of Jesus at the end of the first century B.C. It is possible that he says this in answer to the speculations about Adam found in the work of Philo of Alexandria. (He was a Jewish philosopher who lived during the first half of the first century A.D. His aim was to harmonize the Scriptures with Greek thought. Apollos (see 1: 12) came from Alexandria and may have acquainted the Corinthian Christians with the kind of Jewish philosophy current there.) In his exposition of the two creation stories in Gen. 1 and 2, Philo claimed that the first account of the creation of man did not refer to the making of Adam (described in Gen. 2), but to another being, a Heavenly Man, who was the pattern or the ideal of humanity and who existed at the beginning, at the same time as Adam. This notion of a Heavenly Man, applied to Christ, could lead to a denial of the importance of Jesus as an historical figure.

50–2. The idea of resurrection as the bringing back to life of our present physical bodies is incorrect: *flesh and blood can never possess the kingdom of God*. This assertion might, however, raise in the readers' minds the question of what exactly was going to happen to Christians who were still alive on this earth at the coming of Christ. Would they have to die first, in order to enter upon the new form of existence? Paul denies this. Those who are still alive will simply undergo some miraculous transformation.

54–5. The origin of the first quotation is obscure. The second comes from Hos. 13: 14.

56–7. *Death* is here represented as an evil creature such as a scorpion. It has a *sting* which enables it to destroy its victims. This sting is *sin*. In other words, because men fall under the control of sin they also die (Rom. 6: 23). Paul adds: *sin gains its power from the law*. In Rom. 7: 7–11 he explains that a knowledge of the moral laws which ought to govern human behaviour simply showed him what sin was, and produced in him a desire to commit the forbidden action. However, he firmly believes that this whole tragic situation has been remedied by Christ. ✲

Christian Giving

AND NOW ABOUT the collection in aid of God's **16** people: you should follow my directions to our congregations in Galatia. Every Sunday each of you is to **2** put aside and keep by him a sum in proportion to his gains, so that there may be no collecting when I come. When I arrive, I will give letters of introduction to per- **3** sons approved by you, and send them to carry your gift to Jerusalem. If it should seem worth while for me to go **4** as well, they shall go with me.

5 I shall come to Corinth after passing through Mace-
6 donia—for I am travelling by way of Macedonia—and I
may stay with you, perhaps even for the whole winter,
and then you can help me on my way wherever I go next.
7 I do not want this to be a flying visit; I hope to spend
8 some time with you, if the Lord permits. But I shall
9 remain at Ephesus until Whitsuntide, for a great opportunity has opened for effective work, and there is much
opposition.

10 If Timothy comes, see that you put him at his ease;
for it is the Lord's work that he is engaged upon, as I am
11 myself; so no one must slight him. Send him happily on
his way to join me, since I am waiting for him with our
12 friends. As for our friend Apollos, I urged him strongly
to go to Corinth with the others, but he was quite determined not to go at present; he will go when opportunity offers.

13 Be alert; stand firm in the faith; be valiant and strong.
14 Let all you do be done in love.

15 I have a request to make of you, my brothers. You
know that the Stephanas family were the first converts in
Achaia, and have laid themselves out to serve God's
16 people. I wish you to give their due position to such
persons, and indeed to everyone who labours hard at our
17 common task. It is a great pleasure to me that Stephanas,
Fortunatus, and Achaicus have arrived, because they have
done what you had no chance to do; they have relieved
18 my mind—and no doubt yours too. Such men deserve
recognition.

19 Greetings from the congregations in Asia. Many
greetings in the Lord from Aquila and Prisca and the

congregation at their house. Greetings from all the 20
brothers. Greet one another with the kiss of peace.

This greeting is in my own hand—PAUL.   21

If anyone does not love the Lord, let him be outcast.   22
Marana tha—Come, O Lord!
The grace of the Lord Jesus Christ be with you.   23
My love to you all in Christ Jesus. Amen.   24

✻ 1. On the occasion of his second visit to Jerusalem after
his conversion, Paul had promised the leading apostles there
that he would do what he could to help their poorer members
(Gal. 2: 10). In fulfilment of this promise he had organized a
collection in aid of God's people to which the churches he had
founded were to contribute. It is mentioned in Rom. 15: 26,
where we read that the congregations of Macedonia and
Achaia have 'resolved to raise a common fund for the benefit
of the poor among God's people at Jerusalem', and in 2 Cor.
9: 2 it is said that the Corinthian Christians are especially keen
to help with the project.

9. *Whitsuntide* refers to the Jewish Feast of Pentecost (not
to the later Christian festival). The term is used here by the
translators to give some rough indication of the time of year
Paul has in mind.

10–11. Some of the Corinthians were inclined to disregard
the authority of Paul himself. They might well show even less
respect to *Timothy*, who was younger in age and junior in
status.

12. This may be a mild reminder to those of the 'Apollos
party' that *Apollos* himself by no means approved of their
partisanship. If he were eager to increase his own personal
influence in the church at Corinth he would surely have been
more ready to pay them a visit. It also serves to show the
adherents of 'Paul's party' that the work of Apollos has Paul's
support, otherwise he would not have *urged him strongly to
go to Corinth*.

15. For *Stephanas*, see 1: 16.

19. See Acts 18: 2–3, 26 for information about *Aquila and Prisca* (Priscilla in Acts). They had been forced to leave Rome as a result of Claudius' edict of A.D. 49 which expelled the Jews from the city. They appear to have carried on their trade, that of tent-making, both in Corinth and in Ephesus.

20. The *kiss of peace* is simply an expression of brotherly love among the members of the congregation, although in later centuries it was sometimes a part of formal worship. The second-century writer Justin says that the kiss was given to the newly baptized converts before they took part in the Eucharist (i.e. the Lord's Supper).

21–4. The letter as a whole will have been dictated by Paul to one of his companions, acting as his secretary. The concluding greetings he writes himself (see p. 13).

22. *Marana tha* is a very early Christian prayer in Aramaic, used originally in the churches in Palestine. When it was passed on to the Greek-speaking churches it remained untranslated. As the N.E.B. shows, it means *Come, O Lord!* Obviously it refers to Christ, but its more exact significance is not so clear. It may be a prayer that the return of Christ at the end of the world may not be long delayed. Alternatively, it may be a petition for the invisible presence of Christ at gatherings for Christian worship. In the *Didache*, a second-century book containing, among other things, instructions for the conduct of services, *Marana tha* is found at the end of a version of the prayer to be said at the Eucharist. ✳

✳ ✳ ✳ ✳ ✳ ✳ ✳ ✳ ✳ ✳ ✳ ✳ ✳

THE SECOND LETTER OF PAUL TO THE CORINTHIANS

EVENTS FOLLOWING THE WRITING OF I CORINTHIANS

(i) Paul paid a second visit to Corinth. His first visit was when he founded the church there (see p. 2). This first visit was followed by a letter which his readers misunderstood (1 Cor. 5: 9–10) and which some scholars suppose to have been preserved in 2 Cor. 6: 14 — 7: 1. He then wrote our present 1 Corinthians. We know that after this he paid a second visit, because in 2 Cor. 12: 14 he says that he is about to come for the third time (see also 2 Cor. 13: 1). He also implies that his second personal encounter with them had been a rather unpleasant experience. In 2 Cor. 2: 1 he says that his next visit (i.e. the third) must not be 'another painful one'. This suggests that one of their two previous meetings had been 'painful'. 1 Corinthians gives no sign that it was the first visit of all which had been unpleasant, so it must have been the second which had proved distressing. We may conjecture that it took place because Paul (working in Ephesus) heard disturbing news from Corinth which made him decide to see for himself what was happening. It has been suggested that his converts were being influenced, and that his own authority was being undermined, by missionaries from elsewhere. These would be the people whom he calls 'sham-apostles...masquerading as apostles of Christ' (2 Cor. 11: 13).

(ii) While he was in Corinth on this second occasion, or just after he had left the city, some member of the congregation committed an act of indiscipline. No one knows what it was, but obviously Paul felt that it had injured the whole community. It may have been personally insulting to himself as well, although he does not stress this. It is perhaps better to suppose that this act of defiance occurred after his departure.

He attempted to reassert his authority by letter (see below). He would not have done this if he had had the opportunity of dealing with the offender in person on the spot, for writing would have provided excellent ammunition for those of his opponents who accused him of being 'feeble' when he was 'face to face' with them and 'brave' when he was away (see 2 Cor. 10: 1, 9–11). If he had already left Corinth, the personal insult to his authority must have been offered to one of his assistants, such as Timothy.

(iii) Paul decided not to visit Corinth again for the time being but to deal with the situation by means of a letter. Its composition caused him much distress, but it seems to have achieved its object (see 2 Cor. 2: 1–6). Some scholars think that it has been preserved as chapters 10–13 of our present 2 Corinthians.

(iv) Titus was sent to Corinth, either as the bearer of the letter or shortly afterwards to see what the effect of it had been.

(v) At roughly the same time as these events Paul himself had been in great danger of death (see 2 Cor. 1: 8–10), either as a result of severe illness or alternatively because he was suffering violent persecution.

(vi) Later he left Ephesus for Troas, the port from which one sailed to Macedonia. Here he had expected Titus to meet him, with news from Corinth, but since Titus had not arrived he crossed over to Macedonia himself.

(vii) There he at last encountered Titus, who had an encouraging report to give him (see 2 Cor. 7: 5–16). This meeting was followed by the writing of 2 Corinthians (or chapters 1–9 of our present 2 Corinthians, if we suppose that chapters 10–13 are part of the earlier letter).

See pp. 3–13 for a detailed discussion of the different letters Paul wrote to the Corinthians. We can give a brief outline of his letters and of his visits to Corinth as follows:

First visit (foundation of the church).

First letter (perhaps lost, perhaps preserved in 2 Cor. 6: 14 — 7: 1).

1 Corinthians.
Second visit (the 'painful visit').
'Painful letter' (perhaps preserved in 2 Cor. 10–13).
(Paul reaches Macedonia.)
2 Corinthians (or 2 Cor. 1–9, perhaps with the exception of
6: 14 — 7: 1).

✳   ✳   ✳   ✳   ✳   ✳   ✳   ✳   ✳   ✳   ✳   ✳   ✳

Personal Religion and
the Ministry

OPENING REMARKS

F ROM PAUL, apostle of Christ Jesus by God's will, and **1**
our colleague Timothy, to the congregation of God's
people at Corinth, together with all who are dedicated to
him throughout the whole of Achaia.

Grace and peace to you from God our Father and the ₂
Lord Jesus Christ.

Praise be to the God and Father of our Lord Jesus Christ, ₃
the all-merciful Father, the God whose consolation never
fails us! He comforts us in all our troubles, so that we ₄
in turn may be able to comfort others in any trouble of
theirs and to share with them the consolation we ourselves
receive from God. As Christ's cup of suffering overflows, ₅
and we suffer with him, so also through Christ our
consolation overflows. If distress be our lot, it is the price ₆
we pay for your consolation, for your salvation; if our
lot be consolation, it is to help us to bring you comfort,
and strength to face with fortitude the same sufferings we

7 now endure. And our hope for you is firmly grounded; for we know that if you have part in the suffering, you have part also in the divine consolation.

8   In saying this, we should like you to know, dear friends, how serious was the trouble that came upon us in the province of Asia. The burden of it was far too heavy for 9 us to bear, so heavy that we even despaired of life. Indeed, we felt in our hearts that we had received a death-sentence. This was meant to teach us not to place reliance 10 on ourselves, but on God who raises the dead. From such mortal peril God delivered us; and he will deliver us again, he on whom our hope is fixed. Yes, he will con-11 tinue to deliver us, if you will co-operate by praying for us. Then, with so many people praying for our deliverance, there will be many to give thanks on our behalf for the gracious favour God has shown towards us.

✳ After the opening greeting, the letter continues with the usual thanksgiving. Unlike the beginning of 1 Corinthians, this is concerned not with the spiritual progress of Paul's correspondents but with his own recent escape from mortal danger.

4, 6. Nevertheless, the thanksgiving has some connexion with his readers. God gave him inward strength to endure his suffering, but this was not for himself alone, but so that he should know how to *comfort* others who might be overwhelmed by similar distress.

5. The experiences of Jesus are shared by his followers. Jesus himself suggested that they might have to face death as a result of their loyalty to him when he said, 'Anyone who wishes to be a follower of mine...must take up his cross, and come with me' (Mark 8: 34). Paul believed that there was so close a unity between Christ and Christians that Christians could be thought of as sharing Christ's own personality. This

meant that what had happened to Christ became part of their own experience and that, in turn, their own experience reproduced his. Just as Christ had suffered the impact of evil in all its forms, betrayal, injustice, cruelty, intense physical pain, and finally death, so Christians would in some degree have to *suffer* these things *with him*. But just as Christ had not been destroyed by the power of evil, but had been raised from the dead, *so also*, as Paul puts it from his own personal point of view, *through Christ our consolation overflows*. He had himself been rescued from danger by *God who raises the dead* (verse 9). Christ's experience of the life-giving power of God, as well as his experience of suffering, is reproduced in the experience of his followers.

8. Opinions differ as to what this *trouble* was. It has been suggested that Paul had fallen seriously ill. Later in 2 Corinthians he refers to a disease which attacked him from time to time and which appeared incurable (12: 7–9). But if this is what he is alluding to it is surely rather strange that he should use the first person plural, *us*. In the later reference he speaks, as one would naturally expect, in the first person singular. It is more reasonable to suppose that he is referring to suffering in which his companions had also been involved, even if to a lesser degree. In that case, the trouble was probably some particularly severe experience of persecution. *

A CHANGE OF PLAN

There is one thing we are proud of: our conscience 12 assures us that in our dealings with our fellow-men, and above all in our dealings with you, our conduct has been governed by a devout and godly sincerity, by the grace of God and not by worldly wisdom. There is nothing in 13 our letters to you but what you can read for yourselves, and understand too. Partial as your present knowledge of 14 us is, you will I hope come to understand fully that you have as much reason to be proud of us, as we of you, on the Day of our Lord Jesus.

15 It was because I felt so confident about all this that I had intended to come first of all to you and give you the
16 benefit of a double visit: I meant to visit you on my way to Macedonia, and after leaving Macedonia, to return to you, and you would then send me on my way to Judaea.
17 That was my intention; did I lightly change my mind? Or do I, when I frame my plans, frame them as a worldly man might, so that it should rest with me to say 'yes' and
18 'yes', or 'no' and 'no'? As God is true, the language in which we address you is not an ambiguous blend of Yes
19 and No. The Son of God, Christ Jesus, proclaimed among you by us (by Silvanus and Timothy, I mean, as well as myself), was never a blend of Yes and No. With him it
20 was, and is, Yes. He is the Yes pronounced upon God's promises, every one of them. That is why, when we give glory to God, it is through Christ Jesus that we say
21 'Amen'. And if you and we belong to Christ, guaranteed
22 as his and anointed, it is all God's doing; it is God also who has set his seal upon us, and as a pledge of what is to come has given the Spirit to dwell in our hearts.

✳ Throughout this letter Paul finds it necessary to defend himself against adverse criticism. Here it is against a charge of inconsistency, of making plans and then changing his mind and failing to carry them out.

13. His letters are to be taken at their face value. They carry no hidden undertones which contradict their surface meaning.

15–16. This travel plan differs from the one suggested in the closing paragraphs of 1 Corinthians (16: 5–7). Here Paul says that he had originally intended to visit Corinth briefly before going on to Macedonia, whereas in 1 Corinthians he had proposed to stay in Corinth only after passing through Macedonia first. However, this is not the change of plan that his correspondents are now complaining about. They are now complaining that he has not fulfilled his intention of visiting them on his *way to Macedonia*. We are probably to assume that some considerable interval of time has elapsed since the writing of 1 Corinthians, and that the plan outlined there has been forgotten both by Paul and by the Corinthians.

17. The first point he makes by way of reply is that whatever plans he has made he has not made them *as a worldly man might*, implying that, on the contrary, they have been framed in accordance with God's intentions, not his own. It has not rested with Paul himself to decide to do a thing or not to do it.

18. Secondly, he has not been insincere or hypocritical in what he has said or written.

19. This is because the conduct of Christ's apostles must imitate the conduct of Christ himself, and the character of Jesus is totally opposed to any kind of double-dealing whereby a man says one thing but means another. The underlying thought is that Jesus was completely obedient to the will of God, and God himself is always consistent. He always means what he says, and always says 'Yes' to his own promises of what he will do, i.e. he always carries out his promises. Since Jesus always obeyed God it can therefore be said of Jesus also: *With him it was, and is, Yes.*

20. It is Jesus who actually fulfils God's promises, says *Yes* to them. These promises were made known through the prophets in the course of the history of Israel. All Christians firmly believed that the Old Testament prophecies were predictions about Jesus, and that they came true as a result of what he did and what happened to him. Because Jesus freely accepted the will of God, God's plan for himself, it is in the name of Christ that Christians, at the end of their prayers, assert their own acceptance of God's will by saying '*Amen*', i.e. 'So let it be'.

21-2. They can do this only because they *belong to Christ*. It is because they are members of the Body of Christ that his personal qualities of character are transmitted to them and that they are therefore able to reproduce the actions of Jesus in their own lives. The assertion that their relationship to Christ *is all God's doing* does not seem to have any close connexion with the preceding argument. It is possibly to be understood as a kind of thanksgiving. The description of Christians as *anointed* means, first, that they are followers of the Messiah, the Anointed One, and members of his community. Secondly, it means that they are those to whom God *has given the Spirit*. In the Old Testament narratives the gift of the Spirit sometimes follows actual anointing with oil, as when Samuel anointed David (1 Sam. 16: 13). The reception of the Spirit of God can also be spoken of metaphorically as an anointing (Isa. 61: 1). The chief characteristic of the Messiah is his possession of the Spirit. The further description of them as those upon whom God *has set his seal* means that they have been marked out as his special property. ✶

EXPLANATION OF THE WRITER'S CHANGE OF MIND

23 I appeal to God to witness what I am going to say; I stake my life upon it: it was out of consideration for you that I
24 did not after all come to Corinth. Do not think we are dictating the terms of your faith; your hold on the faith is secure enough. We are working with you for your own
2 happiness. So I made up my mind that my next visit to
2 you must not be another painful one. If I cause pain to you, who is left to cheer me up, except you, whom I have
3 offended? This is precisely the point I made in my letter: I did not want, I said, to come and be made miserable by the very people who ought to have made me happy; and I had sufficient confidence in you all to know that for me

to be happy is for all of you to be happy. That letter 4
I sent you came out of great distress and anxiety; how
many tears I shed as I wrote it! But I never meant to
cause you pain; I wanted you rather to know the love,
the more than ordinary love, that I have for you.

✳ Paul's failure to carry out his promise to visit Corinth was
due to the obscure act of indiscipline committed by some
member of the congregation. He preferred to deal with it by
letter, not because he was a weak character but because he
attached great importance to his personal relationship with his
converts and to the preservation of mutual affection between
himself and them. If he were to visit them before the offence
had been dealt with he would probably be angry with them,
or at any rate very severe. ✳

THE OFFENCE AND ITS CONSEQUENCES

Any injury that has been done, has not been done to me; 5
to some extent, not to labour the point, it has been done
to you all. The penalty on which the general meeting has 6
agreed has met the offence well enough. Something very 7
different is called for now: you must forgive the offender
and put heart into him; the man's sorrow must not be
made so severe as to overwhelm him. I urge you there- 8
fore to assure him of your love for him by a formal act.
I wrote, I may say, to see how you stood the test, whether 9
you fully accepted my authority. But anyone who has 10
your forgiveness has mine too; and when I speak of
forgiving (so far as there is anything for me to forgive),
I mean that as the representative of Christ I have forgiven
him for your sake. For Satan must not be allowed to get 11
the better of us; we know his wiles all too well.

✳ 5–6. Two questions arise here: what was the offence, and what was the penalty which had been imposed as a result of Paul's letter? There is no certain answer to either problem. The offence was something that might have been interpreted as a personal insult to Paul himself. If this were not so, why should he be so careful to insist that it is not the individual and personal aspect which is of importance (verses 5 and 10)? But it has also had an effect upon the life of the whole community. It may have been an attack upon Paul's authority as an apostle, since this would not only injure him personally, but would also raise doubts as to whether the Christian congregation which he had founded at Corinth was genuinely part of the Church. The penalty may have been a sentence of temporary expulsion from the community.

7–8. If the penalty was excommunication, Paul is here recommending the readmission of the offender, by some *formal* ceremony, to the celebration of the Eucharist. It was this service which particularly symbolized the unity of the congregation.

11. One of the major purposes of the mission of Jesus was to teach a man to love his neighbour and so to unite those who were separated from each other by mutual hostility. *Satan* is thought of as the great adversary of Christ, attempting to thwart his plans. One obvious way of doing so would be to promote disunity within a Christian congregation. The Corinthians would therefore be playing into Satan's hands by continuing to exclude the offender from their community life. ✳

TRANSITION TO A FRESH TOPIC

12 Then when I came to Troas, where I was to preach the gospel of Christ, and where an opening awaited me for the
13 Lord's work, I still found no relief of mind, for my colleague Titus was not there to meet me; so I took leave of
14 the people there and went off to Macedonia. But thanks

be to God, who continually leads us about, captives in Christ's triumphal procession, and everywhere uses us to reveal and spread abroad the fragrance of the knowledge of himself! We are indeed the incense offered by Christ 15 to God, both for those who are on the way to salvation, and for those who are on the way to perdition: to the latter it 16 is a deadly fume that kills, to the former a vital fragrance that brings life. Who is equal to such a calling? At least we 17 do not go hawking the word of God about, as so many do; when we declare the word we do it in sincerity, as from God and in God's sight, as members of Christ.

✳ Paul's account of his recent actions breaks off in verse 13 and is not resumed until 7: 5. He begins a description of the work and the message of the apostles which, with a few digressions, lasts until the end of chapter 6.

13. *Titus* is mentioned also in Gal. 2: 1, 3 as one of Paul's companions on his second or third visit to Jerusalem. We hear nothing of him in Acts. According to the Letter of Paul to Titus he later played some part in organizing church life in Crete. Although this letter was probably not written by Paul himself it may contain reliable tradition about what Titus had done.

14. Perhaps it is the subconscious recollection of the good news which Titus had eventually brought (7: 6) which produces the formula of thanksgiving. This evokes other ideas in the writer's mind and brings about the change of subject. Christ is here pictured as a victorious Roman general, holding a *triumphal procession* on his return from battle. The picture may have been suggested by the theme of the contest between Christ and Satan which has been hinted at in verse 11. The apostles, less suitably, are represented as the general's prisoners of war, possibly because Paul thinks of Christians as the slaves of Christ (1 Cor. 7: 22). At any rate, this leads on naturally enough to a consideration of the apostles' function.

15-16. The preaching of the apostles has a radically differen effectt upon different people. To those who are disposed to believe them, *those who are on the way to salvation*, it opens up the possibility of a new and better kind of existence, *life* of a more *vital* and satisfying quality than anything hitherto experienced, life, moreover, that is not to be extinguished by physical death. But to those who are inclined to reject the Gospel, *those who are on the way to perdition*, it is simply a further opportunity for rejecting God's claim to their obedience. It is an occasion for separating themselves from God and sentencing themselves to spiritual death in this life and the possibility of complete annihilation in the end. The metaphor of *incense*, applied to the apostles, suggests that they view their work as a sacrificial offering made to God (the burning of incense accompanied the offering of sacrifice in Jewish ritual). It is, however, an offering made *by Christ*, since it is Christ who inspires and directs their preaching.

17. To *go hawking the word of God about* would be to preach for financial profit, or perhaps for some less obvious form of personal advantage such as securing power over other people's lives. ✳

APOSTOLIC CREDENTIALS

3 Are we beginning all over again to produce our credentials? Do we, like some people, need letters of
2 introduction to you, or from you? No, you are all the letter we need, a letter written on our heart; any man can
3 see it for what it is and read it for himself. And as for you, it is plain that you are a letter that has come from Christ, given to us to deliver: a letter written not with ink but with the Spirit of the living God, written not on stone tablets but on the pages of the human heart.

4 It is in full reliance upon God, through Christ, that we
5 make such claims. There is no question of our being

qualified in ourselves: we cannot claim anything as our own. Such qualification as we have comes from God; it 6 is he who has qualified us to dispense his new covenant— a covenant expressed not in a written document, but in a spiritual bond; for the written law condemns to death, but the Spirit gives life.

✴ Although we cannot know for certain what the exact situation was, it looks as though strangers had come to Corinth with impressive *letters of introduction* from churches elsewhere, and were trying to discredit Paul himself. His answer is the one he has given before (1 Cor. 9: 2). The very existence of the Christian community in Corinth proves that he is an accredited apostle.

2. The Corinthian Christians themselves are his letter of introduction, *a letter written on our heart*. The idea here is that a letter of introduction serves not only to accredit its bearer in the eyes of other people but also to give confidence to the bearer himself. Paul's inward recollection, in moments of doubt or despair, of his successful work in Corinth gives him comfort and reassurance. It is a memory which he possesses in his heart all the time, not something which he can lose as one might lose an actual letter.

3–6. The metaphor of the letter is extended and given further meaning. The church in Corinth is *a letter that has come from Christ*. Christ uses his followers to make contact with those who know nothing about him. Their existence as a community is a kind of message to the outside world. Also, they are a letter *given to* the apostles *to deliver*. This emphasizes the fact that it is Christ who is the real founder of the Corinthian church. The apostles are like postmen who deliver letters they have not themselves written. They are necessary as assistants and intermediaries, but it is not they who take the initiative in the first place. Furthermore, the letter is *written not with ink but with the Spirit of the living God.* Paul's preaching at Corinth, by which, humanly speaking, the Christian church there came into existence, was effective because it was motivated and directed by the Spirit of God.

This remark in turn calls to mind one of the major differences between the Jewish faith and Christianity, between the former relationship between God and his people (the old covenant) and the present relationship established by Christ (the *new covenant*). In our terms this would be the difference between the religion of the Old Testament and the religion of the New. In Old Testament times God made his commands known to his people by means of *a written document*, the Law of Moses, inscribed (so the Jews believed) *on stone tablets*. If a Jew wished to know what God wanted him to do he had to refer to this written code of religion and morals. He did not know what God's instructions were without, so to say, consulting his book of reference. This also meant that the relationship between himself and God was rather impersonal and second-hand. Since the coming of Christ, however, God makes his commands known through the inward guidance of the Holy Spirit. The Christian does not need to refer to a written code of laws. For him, God's instructions are inscribed *on the pages of the human heart*; he knows inwardly what God wants him to do. This fulfils Jeremiah's prediction concerning the new relationship between God and his people which was to come into being at some point in the future: 'But this is the covenant that I will make with the house of Israel after those days, saith the Lord; I will put my law in their inward parts, and in their heart will I write it' (Jer. 31: 33). And the new relationship is a personal, first-hand one, *a spiritual bond*. Lastly, the difference between the old covenant and the new is that *the written law condemns to death, but the Spirit gives life*. The written code of morals showed men what sinful conduct was, and the punishment for it, but it failed to give them any power to avoid committing the forbidden actions. It even seemed to provoke them, by clearly describing what they were. Paul would not have known what coveting meant, if this had not been explained in the Law (Rom. 7: 7). It therefore brought with it death, the final penalty for sin (1 Cor. 15: 56). But those who are inspired by the Spirit of God not only know what God's commands are but also possess the inward power to obey them. Therefore death in their case will not have the last word. Their eventual destiny is eternal life. ✳

THE OLD ORDER AND THE NEW

The law, then, engraved letter by letter upon stone, dispensed death, and yet it was inaugurated with divine splendour. That splendour, though it was soon to fade, made the face of Moses so bright that the Israelites could not gaze steadily at him. But if so, must not even greater splendour rest upon the divine dispensation of the Spirit? If splendour accompanied the dispensation under which we are condemned, how much richer in splendour must that one be under which we are acquitted! Indeed, the splendour that once was is now no splendour at all; it is outshone by a splendour greater still. For if that which was soon to fade had its moment of splendour, how much greater is the splendour of that which endures!

With such a hope as this we speak out boldly; it is not for us to do as Moses did: he put a veil over his face to keep the Israelites from gazing on that fading splendour until it was gone. But in any case their minds had been made insensitive, for that same veil is there to this very day when the lesson is read from the old covenant; and it is never lifted, because only in Christ is the old covenant abrogated. But to this very day, every time the Law of

Moses is read, a veil lies over the minds of the hearers.
16 However, as Scripture says of Moses, 'whenever he turns
17 to the Lord the veil is removed'. Now the Lord of whom
this passage speaks is the Spirit; and where the Spirit of
18 the Lord is, there is liberty. And because for us there
is no veil over the face, we all reflect as in a mirror the
splendour of the Lord; thus we are transfigured into his
likeness, from splendour to splendour; such is the influence
of the Lord who is Spirit.

✳ These paragraphs emphasize the superiority of the new
situation, a situation characterized by the fact that Christians
possess the inward guidance of the Spirit of God. Even the old
order of things was splendid and impressive. The religion of
the Jews was by far superior to the cults of the Gentiles.
Nevertheless, the new order is more splendid still, and its
superiority reveals itself several in ways. Under the old order
men inevitably broke God's laws, being powerless to do anything else, and so were *condemned*. Under the new order *we
are acquitted*. Christ has secured forgiveness for us, and the
inward power of the Spirit enables us to obey God, so that
we need not fear condemnation in the future. Also, the old
order was only temporary. The new and personal relationship between God and man which has been inaugurated by
Christ *endures*. Lastly, there is a more direct contact between
God and man under the new order than under the old.

It is possible that the people whose influence at Corinth
Paul feared were Jewish Christians who criticized him for
failing to make his Gentile converts observe the Law of Moses.
This might be the reason why he is trying to prove that
Christianity is different from the Jewish religion and greatly
superior to it. Religion based on the Law of Moses had its
value, but it was a temporary phase in the history of the
relationship between God and man, and it is now super-
seded.

7. The old covenant *was inaugurated with divine splendour.*
See Exod. 24: 16–17. When *Moses* went up Mount Sinai to
receive the Law we are told that 'the glory of the Lord abode
upon mount Sinai'. The 'glory' here means the visible
brightness which was the sign of God's presence: 'And the
appearance of the glory of the Lord was like devouring fire
on the top of the mount.' This was the *splendour* to which the
present verse refers (the Greek word Paul uses, *doxa*, can be
translated by 'glory' as well as by 'splendour'). See also
Exod. 34: 29–35. God's glory was reflected in the face of
Moses after he had spoken with him, so that 'the skin of his
face shone'. The story tells us that the Israelites were not able
to bear the sight of this reflected splendour, and so Moses *put
a veil over his face* until the divine glory died away. In the
following paragraph of his letter (verses 12–18) Paul then takes
the story of the *veil* over the face of Moses and develops it
allegorically in various ways.

12–13. First, it illustrates the fact that the old order was
only temporary and was destined to disappear. The shining of
Moses' face is here taken as a symbol of the splendour of the
Law which Moses had received from God. His purpose in
using the veil is understood to be to prevent the Israelites from
realizing that the glory reflected in his face gradually dis-
appeared. In other words he wished to prevent them from
realizing that the splendour of the Law was a *fading splendour.*
The Christian apostle is in a happier position than Moses was,
since he can *speak out boldly.* Unlike Moses, he does not have
to conceal the fact that the knowledge of God which he
conveys to men is a temporary and incomplete kind of
knowledge, or that the relationship between God and his
people which he helps to bring into existence is an impermanent one.

14–16. Secondly, the veil which hid God's glory from the
Israelites now turns into a symbol of the lack of understanding
on the part of the Jews which has always hidden God and his
purposes from them and which still does hide him from them

in Paul's own day. It is they whose minds are veiled and *insensitive*. They do not realize the true meaning of God's *Law* when they hear it read in the synagogue. To Paul's way of thinking, all the Scriptures were in some way a prophecy of the work of Christ and the new order of things, and so the Law itself pointed to the impermanent nature of the old covenant. But the Jews who refuse conversion to Christianity do not understand this. The veil over their minds *is never lifted, because only in Christ is the old covenant abrogated*. However, should they turn to Christianity their lack of understanding is remedied, and '*the veil is removed*', just as, in the Exodus story, when Moses literally turned to speak with God he took off the veil.

17–18. Thirdly, the veil becomes a more general symbol of lack of direct, face-to-face contact between God and man. For Christians *there is no veil over the face*. They do possess direct contact with God. They see *the splendour of the Lord*. The term 'splendour', or 'glory', which can allude to the visible radiance of God's presence, can also stand for the essential nature and character of God. Christians see God's glory, his essential character, 'in the face of Jesus Christ' (4: 6). Jesus behaves like God, shows us what God is like. Christians therefore have a direct and first-hand knowledge of the nature of God. What is more, just as Moses reflected God's glory in his own face, so Christians reflect in their own lives the character of Christ, and so they *reflect as in a mirror the splendour of the Lord*, i.e. the nature of God himself, and are *transfigured* into the *likeness* of God.

These two verses present us with one very difficult problem, although their general sense is fairly clear. If we look at the more literal translation in the R.V. we see that the first half of verse 17 reads 'Now the Lord is the Spirit'; also, the last phrase in verse 18 is translated 'even as from the Lord the Spirit'. Now the term 'Lord' in Paul's letters usually refers to Christ. If it does so here, these phrases seem to imply that Christ and the Spirit are absolutely identical, with no distinction between them at all. They imply that Christ in his heavenly state, since his resurrection, is the same as the Spirit of God. This conclusion, however, would be contrary not only to the later doctrine of the Trinity but also to the impression produced by Paul's writings as a whole. Elsewhere he speaks frequently both of the work of Christ and of the function of the Spirit, and the use of both terms suggests that they represent separate beings. If he believed quite simply that Christ was the Spirit it would surely prove less confusing to his converts to use one term only.

One possible explanation of the difficulty would be to suppose that in these two verses the word 'Lord' does not, after all, refer to Christ. Verse 16 contains a quotation from the Old Testament where in the original context 'the Lord' refers simply to God. This suggests that in the following verses 'Lord' need not necessarily mean 'Christ'. According to the N.E.B. translation of verse 17, Paul is not making a doctrinal statement which asserts that Christ and the Spirit are the same, but is interpreting the phrase from Exodus which he has just quoted: *Now the Lord of whom this passage speaks is the Spirit.* 'Turning to the Lord' means accepting the new covenant (becoming converted to Christianity), which has previously been described (verse 8) as *the divine dispensation of the Spirit.* When the Jews allow themselves to do this, then *'the veil is removed'.* There is no longer a barrier between themselves and God. They have freedom of access to him, for *where the Spirit of the Lord is, there is liberty.* In this second half of verse 17 'Spirit of the Lord' is the equivalent of 'Spirit of God'. Likewise in verse 18, since Paul still has the Old Testament use of 'Lord' in mind, *the splendour of the Lord* may mean simply 'the glory of God' (again it is not absolutely necessary to suppose that 'Lord' means 'Christ'). The last phrase of the verse could just possibly be translated 'such is the influence of the Spirit of the Lord', which would avoid the identification of Christ and the Spirit. Alternatively, the identification can also be avoided by adopting the N.E.B.

such is the influence of the Lord who is Spirit. Lord can again be used in its Old Testament sense, and the statement that God is *Spirit* fits in well enough with the ideas of the Old Testament. The term *Spirit* signifies 'power', and God himself is the supremely powerful Being. ✶

THE APOSTOLIC MESSAGE AND ITS RECEPTION

4 Seeing then that we have been entrusted with this commission, which we owe entirely to God's mercy, we
2 never lose heart. We have renounced the deeds that men hide for very shame; we neither practise cunning nor distort the word of God; only by declaring the truth openly do we recommend ourselves, and then it is to the common conscience of our fellow-men and in the sight
3 of God. And if indeed our gospel be found veiled, the only people who find it so are those on the way to per-
4 dition. Their unbelieving minds are so blinded by the god of this passing age, that the gospel of the glory of Christ, who is the very image of God, cannot dawn upon them
5 and bring them light. It is not ourselves that we proclaim; we proclaim Christ Jesus as Lord, and ourselves as your
6 servants, for Jesus' sake. For the same God who said, 'Out of darkness let light shine', has caused his light to shine within us, to give the light of revelation—the revelation of the glory of God in the face of Jesus Christ.

✶ Paul insists that the apostles do not carry out their task from any motives of self-interest. He goes on to consider what their message is and how it is received.

2–4. The Christian faith is something which men should naturally accept and believe. It is *the truth*, which should commend itself *to the common conscience* of the apostles' *fellow-men*. Why then do many people refuse to believe it? Part of the answer which Paul would give to this very puzzling question is that it is not entirely a matter of free choice on the part of the unbelievers. They are not left completely to themselves to make the decision. *Their unbelieving minds are... blinded by the god of this passing age.* According to the New Testament view of the world, human beings are not simply left to themselves to live their own lives without interference. They are exposed to the outside influence of non-human spiritual forces and their actions are to some extent determined by this. Ideally, men should be influenced and controlled by God, through the guidance of the Spirit of God. But in actual fact they are more frequently influenced by the powers of evil, that is by Satan and 'the powers that rule the world'.

6. The reference is to Gen. 1: 3, although it is not an exact quotation, since the words of Genesis run, 'And God said, Let there be light'. In the context this is an allusion to the creation of physical light. The *light* Paul is speaking of, however, is the inward spiritual and intellectual illumination which is the result of the knowledge of God's nature which Christians possess through their knowledge of Christ. Paul's comparison of this enlightenment with the original creation of light at the beginning of the world implies that the bringing into existence of Christians by God, through the work of the apostles, is like a fresh creation of the human race. To live as a Christian is a totally new kind of life. ✲

DAILY EXPERIENCE OF DEATH AND LIFE

We are no better than pots of earthenware to contain 7 this treasure, and this proves that such transcendent power does not come from us, but is God's alone. Hard- 8 pressed on every side, we are never hemmed in; bewildered, we are never at our wits' end; hunted, we are 9 never abandoned to our fate; struck down, we are not left to die. Wherever we go we carry death with us in 10

our body, the death that Jesus died, that in this body also
11 life may reveal itself, the life that Jesus lives. For continually, while still alive, we are being surrendered into
the hands of death, for Jesus' sake, so that the life of Jesus
12 also may be revealed in this mortal body of ours. Thus
death is at work in us, and life in you.

13   But Scripture says, 'I believed, and therefore I spoke
out', and we too, in the same spirit of faith, believe and
14 therefore speak out; for we know that he who raised the
Lord Jesus to life will with Jesus raise us too, and bring us
15 to his presence, and you with us. Indeed, it is for your sake
that all things are ordered, so that, as the abounding grace
of God is shared by more and more, the greater may be
the chorus of thanksgiving that ascends to the glory of
God.

✻ The apostles' ability to accomplish their task is not the result
of their own natural capabilities, but is given them by God.
They are just as much exposed to danger and hardship and
human weakness as anyone else—more so than many people.
Nevertheless, in situations where complete defeat and absolute
failure might well be expected as the natural outcome they
continually experience some measure of success and victory.
The suffering and the difficulties they have to contend with
provide occasion for the display of the *transcendent power* which
is God's alone.

7. The comparison with *pots of earthenware* suggests two
ideas. Earthenware pots may contain valuable material, but are
themselves comparatively valueless. They are also easily broken.
The apostles, like the pots, are personally unimportant; it is
what they 'contain', their message, which is the valuable
thing. Like every other human being, the apostles are easily
destroyed by illness or violence or fatal accident.

10–12. See 1: 5. The Christian shares the experiences of

Christ. When the apostles' lives are endangered because of their loyalty to Christ, and when their work involves them in any kind of physical or mental suffering, they share *the death that Jesus died*. (Any form of pain or suffering or weakness was described by the Jews as a kind of death.) But they also share *the life that Jesus lives*. The resurrection of Jesus, his deliverance at God's hands from a situation which appeared to be one of utter defeat and failure and his restoration to continuous life, is reproduced in two aspects of the apostles' experience. First, although Paul and his present companions have suffered to some extent, God has preserved them from worse suffering and indeed from actual death. Secondly, the paradoxical principle that life may emerge as a result of death is illustrated by the fact that the mission of the apostles, which entails a great deal of suffering for themselves, brings life to their converts. They enjoy the new Christian existence which is life of a higher quality than that which they have previously experienced. *Thus death is at work in us, and life in you.*

13. This is quoted from Ps. 116: 10.

14. The Christian's share in Christ's death and resurrection is not confined to the sort of experience within this life which has been already described. Beyond this life he may hope for resurrection in the literal sense of the term (see 1 Cor. 15: 20–2). ✳

LIFE AFTER DEATH

No wonder we do not lose heart! Though our outward 16 humanity is in decay, yet day by day we are inwardly renewed. Our troubles are slight and short-lived; and 17 their outcome an eternal glory which outweighs them far. Meanwhile our eyes are fixed, not on the things that 18 are seen, but on the things that are unseen: for what is seen passes away; what is unseen is eternal. For we know **5** that if the earthly frame that houses us today should be

demolished, we possess a building which God has provided—a house not made by human hands, eternal, and in
2 heaven. In this present body we do indeed groan; we
yearn to have our heavenly habitation put on over this
3 one—in the hope that, being thus clothed, we shall not
4 find ourselves naked. We groan indeed, we who are enclosed within this earthly frame; we are oppressed because we do not want to have the old body stripped off.
Rather our desire is to have the new body put on over it,
so that our mortal part may be absorbed into life im-
5 mortal. God himself has shaped us for this very end; and
as a pledge of it he has given us the Spirit.

6   Therefore we never cease to be confident. We know
that so long as we are at home in the body we are exiles
7 from the Lord; faith is our guide, we do not see him.
8 We are confident, I repeat, and would rather leave our
9 home in the body and go to live with the Lord. We
therefore make it our ambition, wherever we are, here or
10 there, to be acceptable to him. For we must all have our
lives laid open before the tribunal of Christ, where each
must receive what is due to him for his conduct in the
body, good or bad.

* These are some of the most difficult paragraphs in the whole
of Paul's correspondence. There is no general agreement about
how they should be interpreted, and no entirely satisfactory
solution of the problems they raise. Any theory of interpretation is to some extent provisional and incomplete.

We may begin by setting down a number of points upon
which the majority of scholars would probably agree.

(i) For some reason Paul has been led to pay more attention
to the question of what happens to a Christian when he dies.
Previously he had described the condition of the dead as one

of 'sleep' (1 Thess. 4: 13). This was a very common metaphor for death, and he probably used it without thinking what it meant. In any case, when he was writing 1 Thessalonians and 1 Corinthians he seems to have supposed that he himself and the majority of his Christian contemporaries would still be alive when the coming of Christ took place and that they would be immediately transformed into their final state of resurrection glory without having first to undergo the experience of physical death (1 Cor. 15: 51–2; 1 Thess. 4: 15–18). Now he speaks as though they may after all have to die (5: 1). Perhaps it was his own recent escape from death which led his thoughts in this direction (1: 9).

(ii) His general attitude is one of confidence (4: 16–18; 5: 1, 6, 8). It is true that in 5: 4 he perhaps gives the impression that he shrinks from the thought of death, when he says: *we are oppressed because we do not want to have the old body stripped off*. But here he may be expressing the attitude of mind of his readers rather than his own personal view. It is an attitude which he understands and sympathizes with. Perhaps he has shared it at times, but he has succeeded in overcoming it so that he is less troubled by it than they are.

(iii) The fear he is trying to dispel is the fear of those who imagine that after death they will be *naked* (5: 3). This means that when they have been deprived of the 'clothing' of their present bodies they will exist only as disembodied spirits or ghosts. To the Jewish mind this was a condition to be viewed with the greatest apprehension. To be deprived of a body was to be deprived of one's real personality and to become a mere shadow of one's former self. Some of Paul's Greek readers also may have thought of survival after death more in terms of the old myths about the unhappy ghosts in the underworld than in terms of the philosophical theories of the blessedness of the immortal soul freed from the prison of the body. This fear of being deprived of their bodies has led the Corinthians to hope that they may remain alive until the coming of Christ and so may be able to *put on* the resurrection body *over* their present bodies, like putting on one garment over another (5: 2–4). They hope that they need not experience the destruction of their present bodies and a consequent interval of disembodiment, but that their present bodies may be transformed into their resurrection bodies.

(iv) Paul is convinced that death will lead to a closer relationship with Christ (5: 6–8).

It is when we come to consider the way in which he deals with his readers' fear of disembodiment that the greatest disagreement arises. Three possible solutions will be suggested here.

(i) The first verse of chapter 5 can be interpreted to mean that the Christian is transformed into the resurrection state immediately he dies. He is clothed with the resurrection body, the *building which God has provided*, as soon as the *earthly frame* in which he is now 'housed', i.e. his present physical body, is destroyed. There would be no interval between death and resurrection and so no period in which one would remain disembodied. The difficulty here is that this interpretation contradicts what is said in 1 Corinthians. According to 1 Cor. 15: 23, the resurrection of all believers takes place at the same moment, at the coming of Christ. Individual Christians dying at different times do not each experience resurrection as soon as they die. If Paul had changed his mind in the comparatively short interval of time since he wrote 1 Corinthians he would surely have said so, and have explained his new ideas more clearly and fully.

(ii) The present tense, *we possess*, in the first verse of chapter 5 is not to be taken literally. The writer is not suggesting that Christians enter upon the possession of their resurrection bodies at the very moment when their present bodies are destroyed by death. He is simply maintaining that the hope of eventual resurrection is so absolutely certain that his readers need not feel troubled by the prospect of an interval of 'nakedness' between death and the coming of Christ. It is certain that this condition will be only temporary. Moreover, it will have its compensations (5: 6–8). This solution has the merit of simplicity. What is more, it fits in with what is said in I Corinthians. But if this is all that Paul has to say, is it really an adequate answer to his readers' fear of disembodiment? And ought not the present tense in 5: 1 to be taken more seriously?

(iii) The third possible solution is more complicated, but perhaps the most satisfactory in the end. As with the other two, it turns on the interpretation of 5: 1. It has been suggested that the *building which God has provided* is not, after all, the individual resurrection body which is to belong to each Christian eventually. It is a reference to the Body of Christ. This is the image which Paul uses elsewhere to describe the intimate relationship of all Christians with Christ and with each other. It is a relationship which is so close that they can be said to be 'in Christ', and it means that with him they form a single corporate personal unit and share his own personality (see I Cor. 12: 12–31). It would be possible for the image of the building to stand for the image of the Body of Christ, for in I Corinthians the Christian community is described both as 'Christ's body' (12: 27) and as 'God's building' (3: 10).

If this is the correct explanation of 5: 1, Paul is asserting that the relationship of the Christian to Christ (described elsewhere as membership of the Body of Christ) is not something that can be destroyed by physical death. It continues after death, and is *eternal*. Although it is a relationship which begins on earth, it is also *in heaven*, since this is 'where Christ is, seated at the right hand of God' (Col. 3: 1). Therefore it is not affected by our own removal from the earthly scene. In some mysterious way, we ourselves enter Christ's sphere of existence and our personal relationship with him is deepened and intensified. Paul can therefore say that *so long as we are at home in the body* (i.e. so long as we live on this earth) *we are exiles from the Lord*, and that it is preferable to *leave our home in the body and go to live with the Lord* (5: 6, 8; cf. Phil. 1: 21, 23).

But we still have to ask how this interpretation of 5: 1

provides an answer to the fear of disembodiment. We can perhaps see that it does so if we consider what bodily existence meant to the Jews (and Paul was a Jew). They did not think of the physical body as something which enclosed the individual personality and so marked off each human being as separate from every other human being. They held the opposite point of view. To them, the body was the aspect of oneself which made it possible for one person to make contact with another. It is only by using the physical organs of sight, hearing and speech that personal relationships with other people become possible. The body is the means of union with others, not of separation from them. If this is so, then the fear of disembodiment, regarded at a less superficial level, is really the fear of complete loneliness and isolation. It is the fear of being cut off, after death, from all the contacts with others which one had enjoyed while alive on earth. It is apprehension at the thought of being deprived of any real personal life because of the inability to form relationships with other beings. This fear may not be so uncommon as one might suppose. What many people seem to require of life in 'heaven'—if they believe in it—is not the vision of God but the opportunity of reunion with their family and friends. This popular hope may spring from an underlying dread of the opposite condition of solitariness. We die alone. What if we should remain alone, even though in some form we survive? If this is what the fear of disembodiment means, then Paul's answer is a real answer. The personal relationship which matters above everything else, one's relationship with Christ, survives the catastrophe of death and is even intensified in the state beyond death.

There is one possible objection to the interpretation of 5: 1 upon which this third theory depends. In 5: 1 the *building* provided by God and existing *in heaven* has been understood to mean the Body of Christ. But in verse 2 the *heavenly habitation* refers to the individual resurrection body which each Christian is to possess at the coming of Christ. The two terms, *building...in heaven* and *heavenly habitation*, are almost identical. Is it really possible that they can mean two different things? If *heavenly habitation* in verse 2 stands for the individual resurrection body, must we not say that *building...in heaven* in the first verse must also mean this, rather than Body of Christ? And in that case the whole theory breaks down.

We can attempt to solve the difficulty, however, by pointing out that the idea of the resurrection body is not so totally unrelated to the idea of the Body of Christ that it would be impossible for Paul to refer to both ideas in nearly equivalent phrases. The image of the Body of Christ stands for our close relationship with him which can be described as being 'in Christ', and it stands for the fact that Christ in some way shares with his followers his own life and personality. This process begins on earth and will be continued after death. Now our final state of resurrection glory is the result of this process, the final and perfect aspect of our relationship with Christ. It is 'in Christ' that 'all will be brought to life' (1 Cor. 15: 22). And the Christian will possess his resurrection body only as a result of his participation in Christ's own personality: 'He will transfigure the body belonging to our humble state, and give it a form like that of his own resplendent body' (Phil. 3: 21). We may describe the state of the Christian after death (verse 1) as a temporary form of membership of the Body of Christ, and his resurrection state (verse 2) as the final and permanent form of membership. Therefore the use of almost identical images is understandable.

Whichever interpretation of this difficult section we prefer to adopt, one thing is plain. When Paul considers what happens to a person after death he does not think in terms of going to some other place, whether to heaven or to the underworld. What he is concerned about is the Christian's personal relationship with Christ. If this be maintained, as he is convinced it will be, then the Christian need not fear death. Precisely 'where' one will be is a matter of secondary importance.

5. See Rom. 8: 11: 'Moreover, if the Spirit of him who raised Jesus from the dead dwells within you, then the God who raised Christ Jesus from the dead will also give new life to your mortal bodies through his indwelling Spirit.'

10. See 1 Cor. 3: 12–15. ✻

THE NEW ORDER

11 With this fear of the Lord before our eyes we address our appeal to men. To God our lives lie open, as I hope they 12 also lie open to you in your heart of hearts. This is not another attempt to recommend ourselves to you: we are rather giving you a chance to show yourselves proud of us; then you will have something to say to those whose 13 pride is all in outward show and not in inward worth. It may be we are beside ourselves, but it is for God; if we 14 are in our right mind, it is for you. For the love of Christ leaves us no choice, when once we have reached the conclusion that one man died for all and therefore all 15 mankind has died. His purpose in dying for all was that men, while still in life, should cease to live for themselves, and should live for him who for their sake died and was 16 raised to life. With us therefore worldly standards have ceased to count in our estimate of any man; even if once they counted in our understanding of Christ, they do so 17 now no longer. When anyone is united to Christ, there is a new world; the old order has gone, and a new order has already begun.

✻ We return to the subject of the life and work of the apostles. Paul is here trying to help his converts to defend his conduct against outside attack. His defence is twofold. First, he and his fellow-apostles are motivated only by the desire to serve

God and their fellow-men (verse 13). This attitude of self-sacrifice is absolutely demanded because the actions of the Christian must be a replica of the actions of Christ and Christ gave his life for the benefit of mankind (verse 14). This thought leads to the second point. The experiences of Christ are repeated in the experiences of the Christian. The Christian also 'dies', in the sense that the kind of life he lived before his conversion is over and done with; and the Christian is also 'restored to life', in the sense that at his conversion a new kind of existence begins for him (verse 17). The consequence is that his former *worldly standards* of judgement are seen to be worthless. He can no longer estimate a person's character on the basis of *outward show* but must consider his *inward worth*. Now since Paul's opponents profess to be Christians, they ought not to pass judgement on him according to purely human standards as they appear to be doing.

14. The belief that Christ acted representatively on behalf of the whole human race is the key principle of Paul's theology. Because Christ died, the sinful human race whom he represented (verse 21) has in principle been destroyed, so that there is the possibility of a fresh start, *a new world*, for those who are *united to Christ* and so share the life he now possesses (verse 17).

15. They can experience the *new order* so long as they allow their old, self-centred personality to come to an end, i.e. *cease to live for themselves*, and begin to *live for him who for their sake died and was raised to life*.

16. Paul seems to imply that there was a time when he himself applied *worldly standards* to his *understanding of Christ*. Perhaps he is referring to the view of Jesus which he held as a Pharisee before his conversion. He failed to recognize that Jesus was the Messiah appointed by God, and he was therefore looking at him not through God's eyes but through the eyes of the world. If he is including the other apostles with himself, as his use of the first person plural might indicate, he may be recalling the fact that during Jesus' earthly career they

continually expected him to fit in with their own ideas of a Messiah who would wield political and military power, that is, power as the world understands it. ✻

CHRIST'S AMBASSADORS

18 From first to last this has been the work of God. He has reconciled us men to himself through Christ, and he has
19 enlisted us in this service of reconciliation. What I mean is, that God was in Christ reconciling the world to himself, no longer holding men's misdeeds against them, and that he has entrusted us with the message of reconciliation.
20 We come therefore as Christ's ambassadors. It is as if God were appealing to you through us: in Christ's name,
21 we implore you, be reconciled to God! Christ was innocent of sin, and yet for our sake God made him one with the sinfulness of men, so that in him we might be
6 made one with the goodness of God himself. Sharing in God's work, we urge this appeal upon you: you have received the grace of God; do not let it go for nothing.
2 God's own words are:

> 'In the hour of my favour I gave heed to you;
>   On the day of deliverance I came to your aid.'

The hour of favour has now come; now, I say, has the day of deliverance dawned.

✻ The chief function of the apostles is to act as channels of communication between God and the world, to inform men of what God has done for them by means of the mission of Christ. At this point in the letter we have a brief but profound and comprehensive statement of what the action of God was.

18. Briefly summed up, what God has done for us is that *he has reconciled us men to himself.* The Christian faith is funda-

mentally concerned with man's relationship to God. Whatever man may choose to think about it, a relationship of one kind or another does exist. The situation is not one in which each party is content to ignore the other and to remain completely detached. The Epicurean philosophers whom Paul is said to have encountered in Athens (Acts 17: 18) supposed that the gods—if they existed at all—lived far away from the world and took no interest whatsoever in human affairs. This view is very different from the Hebrew and Christian tradition. According to the biblical writers, God may be infinitely distant from man in the sense that he is infinitely holy and powerful. But at the same time he is most intimately concerned with the affairs of humanity. It was God's original intention that man should respond to his love by obeying and trusting him, and so show love to him in return. But this ideal relationship does not in actual fact exist. Man is hostile to God and estranged from him. He neither obeys nor trusts him, but demands complete independence and wants to go his own way. This attitude of mind brings about a state in which God is effectively ignored, and man is no longer conscious of his existence. He may, indeed, produce arguments to prove that God exists, but he can just as easily demolish his proofs by some further exercise of logic. The very fact that he produces proofs shows that no genuine personal relationship exists, at any rate from man's side. One does not need to prove to oneself that one's husband or wife or friend or colleague exists. But although man has chosen to ignore God, God himself has not retaliated by ignoring man. It is his aim to restore the proper relationship between man and himself, to overcome man's hostility and estrangement and to effect a reconciliation. This he has done *in Christ* (verse 19) that is, by sending Christ as his agent.

19, 21. These verses provide a clue to the way in which God reconciled the world to himself. In interpreting Paul, however, we must take two factors into account. First, he is not setting out to provide a detailed and complete explanation of what God has done through Christ, and therefore some of our assumptions about the ideas underlying his remarks, although it is necessary to make them, are somewhat speculative and uncertain. Secondly, some of the views he held and took for granted on such matters as wrongdoing and its penalties may not necessarily fit in with the views which come naturally to us today.

With these considerations in mind we can perhaps explain these two verses as follows. The personal relationship between God and man is not what it should be. Now in ordinary human life a personal relationship can be destroyed in two different ways. It may break down simply because the people concerned become separated from each other geographically. But it can also be ruined by some positive act of wrongdoing committed by one or the other of the parties to it. If a man is discovered to have cheated his partner in business, the friendship which may formerly have existed will come to an end. Indeed, whether or not the injured partner still feels charitably disposed towards the other, the friendship has already been destroyed, as it were unilaterally, by the one who cheated. Already, to do this, he must have ceased to feel friendly towards his partner. And if the broken relationship is to be restored, the man who has done wrong must spontaneously and willingly recognize the fact. He must voluntarily accept the consequences of what he has done, even if this involves suffering some kind of penalty. He must at any rate be willing to accept the penalty, whether or not it is actually imposed upon him. Now the breakdown of the relationship between man and God is of this second kind. Man has sinned against God and has destroyed the personal relationship from his side, even though God still cares for him. In order to put things right, man must willingly accept the consequences of his actions, freely acknowledging that he has been in the wrong. He must show that he recognizes it by being prepared to suffer whatever penalty is necessary. This, however, man is totally unable to do for himself.

Paul maintains that Christ has done this for man, acting as

man's representative. This representation is absolutely real. Christ genuinely experiences our own human situation, a situation in which we are estranged from God. Although he was personally *innocent of sin*, enjoying an unbroken relationship with the Father, nevertheless *God made him one with the sinfulness of men*. He knew what it was like to encounter temptation, and he knew also what it was like to feel himself cut off from the presence of God, as is shown by his cry of despair before he died (Mark 15: 34). But unlike ourselves he freely and willingly accepts the consequences of the sinful situation in which he is involved. He voluntarily suffers death, which Paul thinks of as the consequence of sin and its punishment (Rom. 6: 23). And because of his voluntary acceptance, on our behalf, of the penalties of our wrongdoing, the broken relationship between ourselves and God is repaired. Paul can therefore say that God *no longer* holds *men's misdeeds against them*. Once the results of wrongdoing have been fully faced and accepted, the wrongdoing itself can be forgiven. And because Christ has identified himself with our sinful situation, we in turn may identify ourselves with his *goodness* which belongs to *God himself* and which Christ shares.

6: 1. Paul's converts have experienced the beginning of the new relationship with God brought into effect by Christ. But it will not be automatically maintained, whether they continue to respond or not. It is necessary to urge them, *do not let it go for nothing*.

2. The quotation from Isa. 49: 8 emphasizes the extreme importance of this present period of time in which God has generously chosen to initiate a reconciliation between man and himself. ✶

THE CONDUCT OF THE APOSTLES

In order that our service may not be brought into dis- 3 credit, we avoid giving offence in anything. As God's 4 servants, we try to recommend ourselves in all circum-

stances by our steadfast endurance: in hardships and dire
5 straits; flogged, imprisoned, mobbed; overworked,
6 sleepless, starving. We recommend ourselves by the
innocence of our behaviour, our grasp of truth, our
patience and kindliness; by gifts of the Holy Spirit, by
7 sincere love, by declaring the truth, by the power of God.
We wield the weapons of righteousness in right hand and
8 left. Honour and dishonour, praise and blame, are alike
9 our lot: we are the impostors who speak the truth, the
unknown men whom all men know; dying we still live
10 on; disciplined by suffering, we are not done to death; in
our sorrows we have always cause for joy; poor ourselves,
we bring wealth to many; penniless, we own the world.
11   Men of Corinth, we have spoken very frankly to you;
12 we have opened our heart wide to you all. On our part
there is no constraint; any constraint there may be is in
13 yourselves. In fair exchange then (may a father speak so
to his children?) open wide your hearts to us.

✻ Here we have a description of the harsh life of the apostles
and of the sort of personal behaviour which enables them to
be recognized as *God's servants* despite the difficulties of their
outward circumstances.

11–13. This plea for a response to the writer's affection for
his correspondents takes up again the more strictly personal
theme from which he began to digress in 2: 14, and seems to
lead straight on to 7: 2 and the following paragraphs. ✻

Problems of Church Life
and Discipline

THE SEPARATION OF THE CHURCH FROM THE WORLD

Do NOT UNITE yourselves with unbelievers; they are 14 no fit mates for you. What has righteousness to do with wickedness? Can light consort with darkness? Can 15 Christ agree with Belial, or a believer join hands with an unbeliever? Can there be a compact between the temple 16 of God and the idols of the heathen? And the temple of the living God is what we are. God's own words are: 'I will live and move about among them; I will be their God, and they shall be my people.' And therefore, 'come 17 away and leave them, separate yourselves, says the Lord; do not touch what is unclean. Then I will accept you, says the Lord, the Ruler of all being; I will be a father 18 to you, and you shall be my sons and daughters.' Such are 7 the promises that have been made to us, dear friends. Let us therefore cleanse ourselves from all that can defile flesh or spirit, and in the fear of God complete our consecration.

✶ There are two main reasons for supposing that this paragraph does not belong to the context where we now find it. First, the words in 6: 11, 13, 'we have opened our heart wide to you all...In fair exchange then...open wide your hearts to us', connect very easily with 7: 2, 'Do make a place for us in your hearts!'. There is no immediately obvious connexion between 6: 13 and 6: 14, *Do not unite yourselves with unbelievers.* Secondly, the theme is the avoidance of close contact with the pagan world for fear of becoming involved in its moral corruption. This is not a theme which is dealt with either before or after the present section of the letter. It comes as a complete surprise, and in the context it is irrelevant. It is, of course, possible to find a connexion between 6: 13 and 6: 14 if one tries hard enough. It has been suggested that the Corinthians' attitude of reserve towards Paul is related to their apparent relapse into pagan habits. They may have cooled towards him because they thought he was setting them too high a moral standard. They may then have stopped trying to live up to it, which would make the personal situation worse. If he is to restore the personal relationship he must also deal with the moral corruption. Thus, the theme of the paragraph is not after all irrelevant to its context. If this explanation is plausible, no problem arises. If it seems over-ingenious and unconvincing, we have to explain how the paragraph came to be included in the letter at this point. It may be that Paul was interrupted in the composition of the letter at 6: 13, and that when he began again he had somehow become aware of the need to warn his correspondents against contact with pagans. He did this first, while it was fresh and urgent in his mind, before resuming the theme of personal affection which had been occupying him at the point when he was interrupted. Alternatively, if we are willing to accept that our present 2 Corinthians is a combination of at least two separate letters, and possibly more, it could happen that we have in this paragraph a further short letter, possibly the one mentioned in 1 Cor. 5: 9, or perhaps a part of it.

The insistence that Christians must avoid close contact with *unbelievers* springs from the idea of the Church as a separate community. It is separate because it is the community chosen by God to carry out his purposes in the world (see 1 Cor. 1: 2). Obviously this does not mean that it lives apart from the world, but that it has utterly different standards of behaviour, which must not be compromised.

14. Although a Christian who is already married to an unbeliever is under no obligation to divorce his or her partner

(1 Cor. 7: 12–14), nevertheless it is foolhardy to risk moral corruption by contracting such a marriage where it does not already exist.

15. *Belial* is another name for Satan.

16. This is presumably directed at Christians who feel free to take part in meals held in the temples of *the idols of the heathen* (see 1 Cor. 10: 14–22). For the idea of the Christian community as *the temple of the living God* see 1 Cor. 3: 16. The quotation is a reminiscence of Ezek. 37: 27 and Lev. 26: 12.

17–18. These quotations from the Old Testament are not exact but a combination of odd words and phrases from several of the prophets (see Isa. 43: 6; 52: 11; Jer. 31: 9; 32: 38; 51: 45; Ezek. 20: 34, 41; Hos. 1: 10).

7: 1. The term *flesh* here means the physical body, and *spirit* a person's spiritual and intellectual faculties. Generally in the Pauline writings *flesh* stands for the whole human personality in a state of opposition to God and attachment to the material world (see 1 Cor. 3: 1–4). ✣

PAUL'S PERSONAL NARRATIVE RESUMED

Do make a place for us in your hearts ! We have wronged 2 no one, ruined no one, taken advantage of no one. I do 3 not want to blame you. Why, as I have told you before, the place you have in our heart is such that, come death, come life, we meet it together. I am perfectly frank with 4 you. I have great pride in you. In all our many troubles my cup is full of consolation, and overflows with joy.

Even when we reached Macedonia there was still no 5 relief for this poor body of ours: instead, there was trouble at every turn, quarrels all round us, forebodings in our heart. But God, who brings comfort to the downcast, 6 has comforted us by the arrival of Titus, and not merely 7 by his arrival, but by his being so greatly comforted about

you. He has told us how you long for me, how sorry you
are, and how eager to take my side; and that has made
me happier still.

8   Even if I did wound you by the letter I sent, I do not
now regret it. I may have been sorry for it when I saw
that the letter had caused you pain, even if only for a time;
9 but now I am happy, not that your feelings were wounded
but that the wound led to a change of heart. You bore the
smart as God would have you bear it, and so you are no
10 losers by what we did. For the wound which is borne in
God's way brings a change of heart too salutary to regret;
but the hurt which is borne in the world's way brings
11 death. You bore your hurt in God's way, and see what
its results have been! It made you take the matter
seriously and vindicate yourselves. How angered you
were, how apprehensive! How your longing for me
awoke, yes, and your devotion and your eagerness to see
justice done! At every point you have cleared yourselves
12 of blame in this trouble. And so, although I did send you
that letter, it was not the offender or his victim that most
concerned me. My aim in writing was to help to make
plain to you, in the sight of God, how truly you are
13 devoted to us. That is why we have been so encouraged.

But besides being encouraged ourselves we have also
been delighted beyond everything by seeing how happy
Titus is: you have all helped to set his mind completely at
14 rest. Anything I may have said to him to show my pride
in you has been justified. Every word we ever addressed
to you bore the mark of truth; and the same holds of the
proud boast we made in the presence of Titus: that also
15 has proved true. His heart warms all the more to you as

he recalls how ready you all were to do what he asked, meeting him as you did in fear and trembling. How happy I am now to have complete confidence in you! ₁₆

✻ Paul expresses his deep satisfaction at the response of his correspondents to his previous letter and their change of heart towards him.

5. When he says *there was still no relief for this poor body of ours*, he means much the same thing as when in 2: 13 he says, 'I still found no relief of mind'. The fact that he goes on to mention *trouble at every turn*, *quarrels all round us*, *forebodings in our heart* shows that he is not referring primarily to physical ailments or hardships, although he may have these in mind as well.

5–7. See pp. 119–20 for a summary of the events mentioned here.

8. The *letter* is the same one which has previously been spoken of in 2: 3. It had effected a genuine repentance and so brought about a reconciliation between the writer and his readers. ✻

THE COLLECTION

We must tell you, friends, about the grace of generosity **8** which God has imparted to our congregations in Macedonia. The troubles they have been through have tried ₂ them hard, yet in all this they have been so exuberantly happy that from the depths of their poverty they have shown themselves lavishly open-handed. Going to the ₃ limit of their resources, as I can testify, and even beyond that limit, they begged us most insistently, and on their ₄ own initiative, to be allowed to share in this generous service to their fellow-Christians. And their giving sur- ₅ passed our expectations; for they gave their very selves, offering them in the first instance to the Lord, but also,

6 under God, to us. The upshot is that we have asked Titus, who began it all, to visit you and bring this work of 7 generosity also to completion. You are so rich in every-thing—in faith, speech, knowledge, and zeal of every kind, as well as in the loving regard you have for us—surely you should show yourselves equally lavish in this 8 generous service! This is not meant as an order; by telling you how keen others are I am putting your love to the 9 test. For you know how generous our Lord Jesus Christ has been: he was rich, yet for your sake he became poor, so that through his poverty you might become rich.

10   Here is my considered opinion on the matter. What I ask you to do is in your own interests. You made a good beginning last year both in the work you did and in your 11 willingness to undertake it. Now I want you to go on and finish it: be as eager to complete the scheme as you 12 were to adopt it, and give according to your means. Pro-vided there is an eager desire to give, God accepts what 13 a man has; he does not ask for what he has not. There is no question of relieving others at the cost of hardship 14 to yourselves; it is a question of equality. At the moment your surplus meets their need, but one day your need 15 may be met from their surplus. The aim is equality; as Scripture has it, 'The man who got much had no more than enough, and the man who got little did not go short.'

* Chapters 8 and 9 are both concerned with the collection Paul had undertaken to organize among the Gentile churches for the benefit of the members of the Jerusalem church, who appear to have fallen into a condition of extreme poverty. See the commentary on 1 Cor. 16: 1 for further information. The project had obviously assumed a great deal of importance

in Paul's mind. The conservative Jewish Christian circles in
Jerusalem had frequently shown themselves opposed to his
liberal policy towards Gentiles, in particular to his refusal to
insist that Gentile converts should be circumcised and keep the
Law of Moses. What is more, some of these Jewish Christians
had left Jerusalem and had stirred up trouble in the predomin-
antly Gentile churches, especially the churches of Galatia, by
maintaining that a full observance of the Mosaic Law was
obligatory for all Christians. It was this situation which had
provoked the Letter to the Galatians. Although Paul could not
abandon or compromise his own convictions, nevertheless he
did not wish to be responsible for splitting the Church into
two irreconcilable halves, the one Jewish and the other Gentile.
The collection was to be a means of bringing the two sides
together. It would show that the Gentile Christians did not
wish to hold themselves aloof from their Jewish brothers who
had formed the original nucleus of the Church and to whom,
therefore, they indirectly owed their conversion to Christianity. It was to be an expression of gratitude, and also a proof
that Christian love was just as characteristic of the Gentile as
of the Jewish members of the Church. It looks as though the
church in Jerusalem was poorer than other Christian congregations (8: 13-14). If there is any special reason for this, it may
be that the system of sharing all their goods and property in
common (Acts 2: 44-5; 4: 32-7) had been organized in-
efficiently and had finally broken down. Some people had
disposed of permanent assets such as land and had given the
proceeds to the church. They then relied on the distribution
from the common fund. These Christians would be reduced
to conditions of great hardship if the fund became exhausted.

The Corinthians had begun to contribute their share of the
collection during the previous year, but their enthusiasm seems
to have waned somewhat. Paul tries to encourage them by
quoting the example of the generosity shown by the churches
of Macedonia, and informs them of his intention to send *Titus*
to Corinth to help them with their arrangements.

1. The *congregations in Macedonia* are probably the churches of Thessalonica, Philippi, and Beroea. (See Acts 16: 11 — 17: 15).

2. *The troubles* may have been persecution of some kind. Paul's correspondence with the church at Thessalonica shows that the Thessalonian Christians had been persecuted because of their faith (1 Thess. 2: 14–15; 2 Thess. 1: 4). The *poverty* referred to here was perhaps the result of this. The Macedonian Christians may have been turned out of their jobs or have had their businesses boycotted.

5. They gave their time and interest, as well as their money.

9. The Christian motive for generous giving springs ultimately from the example of Christ himself. As Paul puts it in Phil. 2: 6–7, 'the divine nature was his from the first; yet he did not think to snatch at equality with God, but made himself nothing, assuming the nature of a slave'. For the Son of God to become man meant that, for the benefit of the human race, he was in some sense depriving himself of the infinitely richer form of existence which he already enjoyed.

15. See Exod. 16: 18 (the story of the manna in the desert). ✶

SAFEGUARDS AGAINST CRITICISM

16 I thank God that he has made Titus as keen on your
17 behalf as we are! For Titus not only welcomed our request; he is so eager that by his own desire he is now
18 leaving to come to you. With him we are sending one of our company whose reputation is high among our congregations everywhere for his services to the Gospel.
19 Moreover they have duly appointed him to travel with us and help in this beneficent work, by which we do honour to the Lord himself and show our own eagerness
20 to serve. We want to guard against any criticism of our
21 handling of this generous gift; for our aims are entirely

honourable, not only in the Lord's eyes, but also in the eyes of men.

With these men we are sending another of our com- 22
pany whose enthusiasm we have had many opportunities of testing, and who is now all the more earnest because of the great confidence he has in you. If there is any question 23
about Titus, he is my partner and my associate in dealings with you; as for the others, they are delegates of our congregations, an honour to Christ. Then give them clear 24
expression of your love and justify our pride in you; justify it to them, and through them to the congregations.

About the provision of aid for God's people, it is **9**
superfluous for me to write to you. I know how eager 2
you are to help; I speak of it with pride to the Mace-donians: I tell them that Achaia had everything ready last year; and most of them have been fired by your zeal. My purpose in sending these friends is to ensure that 3
what we have said about you in this matter should not prove to be an empty boast. By that I mean, I want you to be prepared, as I told them you were; for if I bring 4
with me men from Macedonia and they find you are not prepared, what a disgrace it will be to us, let alone to you, after all the confidence we have shown! I have accord- 5
ingly thought it necessary to ask these friends to go on ahead to Corinth, to see that your promised bounty is in order before I come; it will then be awaiting me as a bounty indeed, and not as an extortion.

✻ Two other people, appointed not by Paul himself but by some of the churches he has founded, are to accompany *Titus* on his mission to Corinth. Paul has opponents who might accuse him of trying to make some financial profit for himself, on the pretext of collecting money for the poor. Since Titus is his friend and colleague he also might be suspect. It is therefore necessary to have independent witnesses to prove that there is no question of any private profit. Who these two people were it is impossible to say.

9: 1. The opening of this chapter is rather unexpected. It gives the impression that Paul is only just beginning to talk about the arrangements for the collection, whereas in actual fact he had already devoted several paragraphs to it. It has therefore been suggested that chapters 8 and 9 are to be separated and considered as parts of different letters, later put together because they deal with a common topic. Further evidence for this theory is provided by the fact that in this chapter we read of the enthusiasm of the Corinthians, which has been held up as an example to the churches of Macedonia, and this seems to contradict what is said in chapter 8 about the enthusiasm of the Macedonians which is mentioned as an example for the Corinthians to follow. It is doubtful, however, whether the hypothesis of two separate letters is necessary here. The apparent introduction of the collection as a new topic might be accounted for by supposing that there was some interruption in the composition of the letter at 8: 24. Moreover, although chapter 9 seems at first sight to contradict chapter 8, in reality in both chapters the implied situation in Corinth is the same. Chapter 8 suggests that the Corinthians need to be encouraged to continue with the charitable work they have begun; they are somewhat lacking in eagerness. Now although chapter 9 does speak of their eagerness, it is clear that at the moment of writing Paul doubts very much whether their enthusiasm has come to anything. ✳

FURTHER ENCOURAGEMENT TO GIVE GENEROUSLY

6 Remember: sparse sowing, sparse reaping; sow bounti-
7 fully, and you will reap bountifully. Each person should give as he has decided for himself; there should be no

reluctance, no sense of compulsion; God loves a cheerful
giver. And it is in God's power to provide you richly 8
with every good gift; thus you will have ample means in
yourselves to meet each and every situation, with enough
and to spare for every good cause. Scripture says of such 9
a man: 'He has lavished his gifts on the needy, his
benevolence stands fast for ever.' Now he who provides 10
seed for sowing and bread for food will provide the
seed for you to sow; he will multiply it and swell the
harvest of your benevolence, and you will always be 11
rich enough to be generous. Through our action such
generosity will issue in thanksgiving to God, for as a 12
piece of willing service this is not only a contribution
towards the needs of God's people; more than that, it
overflows in a flood of thanksgiving to God. For through 13
the proof which this affords, many will give honour to
God when they see how humbly you obey him and how
faithfully you confess the gospel of Christ; and will thank
him for your liberal contribution to their need and to the
general good. And as they join in prayer on your behalf, 14
their hearts will go out to you because of the richness of
the grace which God has imparted to you. Thanks be to 15
God for his gift beyond words!

✶ Generous giving on the part of the Corinthians will
eventually be rewarded. God will amply provide for them so
that they will have enough for their own needs and will be
able to give plenty to other people as well (verses 6–11).
What is more, this particular gift will be the means of establishing affectionate relations between the Jerusalem Christians
and the Gentile churches (verse 14). But these are subordinate
motives for Christian *generosity*. Fundamentally it is a response to the inexpressible generosity of God himself. As Paul

puts it in the Letter to the Romans: 'He did not spare his own Son, but surrendered him for us all; and with this gift how can he fail to lavish upon us all he has to give?' (Rom. 8: 32).

9. See Ps. 112: 9. *

Trials of a Christian Missionary

10 BUT I, PAUL, appeal to you by the gentleness and magnanimity of Christ—I, so feeble (you say) when I am face to face with you, so brave when I am away.
2 Spare me, I beg you, the necessity of such bravery when I come, for I reckon I could put on as bold a face as you please against those who charge us with moral weakness.
3 Weak men we may be, but it is not as such that we
4 fight our battles. The weapons we wield are not merely
5 human, but divinely potent to demolish strongholds; we demolish sophistries and all that rears its proud head against the knowledge of God; we compel every human
6 thought to surrender in obedience to Christ; and we are prepared to punish all rebellion when once you have put yourselves in our hands.

7   Look facts in the face. Someone is convinced, is he, that he belongs to Christ? Let him think again, and reflect
8 that we belong to Christ as much as he does. Indeed, if I am somewhat over-boastful about our authority—an authority given by the Lord to build you up, not pull you
9 down—I shall make my boast good. So you must not think of me as one who scares you by the letters he
10 writes. 'His letters', so it is said, 'are weighty and power-ful; but when he appears he has no presence, and as a
11 speaker he is beneath contempt.' People who talk in that

way should reckon with this: when I come, my actions will show the same man as my letters showed in my absence.

* See pp. 5–8 for a discussion of the question whether chapters 10–13 are part of a separate letter. The theme throughout is Paul's defence of his own authority as an apostle and as the founder of the Corinthian church. It is a theme which has occurred elsewhere in both of our present letters, but here it is treated more continuously and vehemently. The apostle's opponents remain anonymous, but they can be described as follows.

(i) They claim to be 'apostles of Christ' (11: 13; see also 10: 7; 11: 5). They were not originally members of the congregation at Corinth but have come from elsewhere (11: 4).

(ii) They have come to a city or a region which has already been evangelized, and when they have worked there for a short time they proceed to take all the credit for the area's conversion to Christianity and the establishment of the church there (10: 12–18).

(iii) They are arrogant, tyrannical, and boastful (10: 12; 11: 18, 20).

(iv) They preach a version of Christianity different from that preached by Paul (11: 4).

(v) They are Jews, and attach a great deal of importance to this fact (11: 22). This point and the previous one suggest that they probably stressed the importance of keeping the Law of Moses and presented Christianity not as something new but as a more advanced form of Judaism, so diminishing the significance of Christ himself.

In these paragraphs Paul defends himself against the charge of being a *weak* character. His opponents accuse him of being unable to make his authority felt when he is actually present in Corinth. He strongly maintains that whether or not he is himself ineffectual, he has more than human power at his disposal for carrying out his task as an apostle. He is empowered and inspired by God (verses 3–5). What is more, he will be as energetic in asserting his authority in person as he appears to be in his letters (verses 9–11). It is an authority which is given him by Christ himself (verse 7).

3–4. Compare 1 Cor. 2: 3–5, for the same contrast between the human weakness to which the apostles are subject like anyone else and the powerful and effective action they are capable of when inspired by God.

5. The *sophistries and all that rears its proud head against the knowledge of God* are probably the same thing as the 'wisdom of this world' which is mentioned in 1 Cor. 1: 20. *Sophistries* are arguments which are superficially clever and impressive, but which are fundamentally misleading and of no value.

6. This verse is rather strange. Surely there will be no need *to punish all rebellion* when the Corinthians have put themselves entirely in Paul's hands, i.e. submitted to his authority? Perhaps *rebellion* refers to the attitude of the intruders. Once Paul has won over the permanent congregation he will be in a stronger position to deal with disturbing influences from outside. *

PAUL'S OWN COMMISSION

12 We should not dare to class ourselves or compare ourselves with any of those who put forward their own claims. What fools they are to measure themselves by themselves, to find in themselves their own standard of 13 comparison! With us there will be no attempt to boast beyond our proper sphere; and our sphere is determined by the limit God laid down for us, which permitted us 14 to come as far as Corinth. We are not overstretching our commission, as we should be if it did not extend to you, for we were the first to reach Corinth in preaching the 15 gospel of Christ. And we do not boast of work done

where others have laboured, work beyond our proper sphere. Our hope is rather that, as your faith grows, we may attain a position among you greater than ever before, but still within the limits of our sphere. Then we can 16 carry the Gospel to lands that lie beyond you, never priding ourselves on work already done in another man's sphere. If a man must boast, let him boast of the Lord. 17 Not the man who recommends himself, but the man 18 whom the Lord recommends—he and he alone is to be accepted.

✻ Paul is perfectly within his rights in asserting his authority in the church at Corinth. He was its human founder, and its foundation was part of the commission given to him by God. By implication, his opponents have no such rights. They are involving themselves in *work beyond* their *proper sphere*. When he speaks in Gal. 1: 16 of what God commissioned him to do, he simply mentions a general mission to the Gentiles without specifying any geographical limitations. Possibly he regarded his sphere of work as limited geographically, first by the fact that he did not work in areas already evangelized by someone else, and secondly by the amount of travel he was actually able to accomplish in regions in which the Christian faith was still unknown.

12. The first half of the verse is obviously sarcastic. The achievements of the 'sham-apostles' are impressive only so long as they are not compared with those of the genuine variety.

16. For a possible explanation of *lands that lie beyond you*, see Rom. 15: 23, where Paul speaks of travelling to Spain after he has visited Rome. ✻

DENUNCIATION OF PAUL'S OPPONENTS

11 I wish you would bear with me in a little of my folly;
2 please do bear with me. I am jealous for you, with a
divine jealousy; for I betrothed you to Christ, thinking
to present you as a chaste virgin to her true and only hus-
3 band. But as the serpent in his cunning seduced Eve, I
am afraid that your thoughts may be corrupted and you
4 may lose your single-hearted devotion to Christ. For
if someone comes who proclaims another Jesus, not the
Jesus whom we proclaimed, or if you then receive a spirit
different from the Spirit already given to you, or a gospel
different from the gospel you have already accepted,
5 you manage to put up with that well enough. Have I
in any way come short of those superlative apostles? I
6 think not. I may be no speaker, but knowledge I have;
at all times we have made known to you the full truth.

7 Or was this my offence, that I made no charge for
preaching the gospel of God, lowering myself to help in
8 raising you? It is true that I took toll of other congrega-
9 tions, accepting support from them to serve you. Then,
while I was with you, if I ran short I sponged on no one;
anything I needed was fully met by our friends who came
from Macedonia; I made it a rule, as I always shall, never
10 to be a burden to you. As surely as the truth of Christ is in
me, I will preserve my pride in this matter throughout
11 Achaia, and nothing shall stop me. Why? Is it that I do
not love you? God knows I do.

12 And I shall go on doing as I am doing now, to cut the
ground from under those who would seize any chance to
put their vaunted apostleship on the same level as ours.

Such men are sham-apostles, crooked in all their practices, 13
masquerading as apostles of Christ. There is nothing sur- 14
prising about that; Satan himself masquerades as an angel
of light. It is therefore a simple thing for his agents to 15
masquerade as agents of good. But they will meet the end
their deeds deserve.

✴ The Corinthians are in danger of changing their fundamental beliefs as a result of the influence of the false apostles.
This is why Paul is so concerned about the weakening of his
own authority.

1. He speaks here of his *folly* because he has just said that
people who put forward their own claims are not to be trusted,
and yet he is himself compelled to do the same thing. But his
motive (unlike that of his opponents) is not really self-recom-
mendation but concern for his converts.

2. The *devotion* of the Christian community to Christ must
be as exclusive as the relationship between wife and husband.
This simile was no doubt suggested by the picture in the Old
Testament of the nation of Israel as the bride of the Lord
(see Hos. 2). The Church has now taken the place of Israel as
God's people, and so inherits the duty of exclusive loyalty to
God. Since Paul has founded the Corinthian church he is
metaphorically in the position of a father who gives his
daughter in marriage. And just as the daughter would be
expected to have remained *a chaste virgin* until she was
married, and so to be morally uncorrupted, so Paul is concerned that his converts should remain uncorrupted in their
beliefs.

3. The story in Gen. 3 describes the spoiling of human life
as it was first created by God. Now it has already been said
(5: 17) that the Christian life is so new and so different from
the pre-Christian life that it is like the creation of a new world.
Paul is afraid lest the influence of the false apostles should spoil

this new world as the serpent in the myth is said to have corrupted the original world.

4. It is not clear what is meant by *another Jesus*. Perhaps the false apostles denied the divinity of Christ. His divinity would have been a difficult idea for many Jews to accept, even if they had been impressed by Jesus' life and teaching and were willing to accept him as the last and greatest of the prophets. It is still less clear how the Corinthians could be said to have received a different *spirit*. In verse 15 the false apostles are described as agents of Satan. Perhaps the idea is that if the Corinthians are influenced by their teaching they may fall under the control of evil spirits.

5. A sarcastic reference to Paul's opponents.

6. It is his own version of the Christian faith which is the *full truth*, not the deviations taught by the false apostles.

7-11. His thoughts turn once more to the fact that he had not accepted financial support from the congregation while he was in Corinth (see 1 Cor. 9). His opponents had presumably fastened on this in order to discredit him in some way. It seems in any case to have been a continual source of misunderstanding. Since it was a Greek custom at this time to accept payment for giving instruction, some people may have said that if Paul charged no fees it was because he knew that his teaching was of little value; he was only an amateur, not professionally qualified. Or was it that inwardly he despised his converts and was too proud to receive support from them? Had he too little affection for them to wish to be under an obligation to them? This last suggestion he vehemently denies. ✷

APOSTOLIC BOASTING

16 I repeat: let no one take me for a fool; but if you must, then give me the privilege of a fool, and let me have my
17 little boast like others. I am not speaking here as a

Christian, but like a fool, if it comes to bragging. So 18
many people brag of their earthly distinctions that I shall
do so too. How gladly you bear with fools, being your- 19
selves so wise! If a man tyrannizes over you, exploits 20
you, gets you in his clutches, puts on airs, and hits you in
the face, you put up with it. And we, you say, have been 21
weak! I admit the reproach.

But if there is to be bravado (and here I speak as a fool),
I can indulge in it too. Are they Hebrews? So am I. 22
Israelites? So am I. Abraham's descendants? So am I.
Are they servants of Christ? I am mad to speak like this, 23
but I can outdo them. More overworked than they,
scourged more severely, more often imprisoned, many
a time face to face with death. Five times the Jews have 24
given me the thirty-nine strokes; three times I have been 25
beaten with rods; once I was stoned; three times I have
been shipwrecked, and for twenty-four hours I was adrift
on the open sea. I have been constantly on the road; I 26
have met dangers from rivers, dangers from robbers,
dangers from my fellow-countrymen, dangers from
foreigners, dangers in towns, dangers in the country,
dangers at sea, dangers from false friends. I have toiled 27
and drudged, I have often gone without sleep; hungry
and thirsty, I have often gone fasting; and I have suffered
from cold and exposure.

Apart from these external things, there is the responsi- 28
bility that weighs on me every day, my anxious concern
for all our congregations. If anyone is weak, do I not 29
share his weakness? If anyone is made to stumble, does
my heart not blaze with indignation? If boasting there 30
must be, I will boast of the things that show up my

31 weakness. The God and Father of the Lord Jesus (blessed be his name for ever!) knows that what I say is true.

32 When I was in Damascus, the commissioner of King Aretas kept the city under observation so as to have me

33 arrested; and I was let down in a basket, through a window in the wall, and so escaped his clutches.

✻ Paul insists that he can equal and surpass his rivals both in *earthly distinctions* (though these do not really count for anything) and in the dangers and hardships he has endured in the course of his work.

22. In so far as these three terms can be distinguished from each other, *Hebrews* emphasizes that Paul and his opponents were by race of Jewish descent (not converts to Judaism, nor half-Jews with only one Jewish parent). *Israelites* stresses that they had been brought up in the Jewish religion, and *Abraham's descendants* that they belonged to the nation to which God had made promises in the past.

23. We know that Paul was *imprisoned* at Philippi (Acts 16: 16–40). The other imprisonments which this verse implies cannot be identified.

24. The Roman authorities allowed the Jews to inflict this punishment upon those of their fellow-Jews who had broken the regulations of the Mosaic Law.

25. The reference to being *beaten with rods* implies punishment at the hands of the Romans themselves. This happened to Paul at Philippi (Acts 16: 22–3). As a Roman citizen he should not have been liable to this penalty, but the Acts narrative shows that mistakes in the administration of justice sometimes occurred. Paul was *stoned* at Lystra (Acts 14: 19).

30. This leads up to the idea expressed in 12: 9–10.

32. See Acts 9: 23–5. In both accounts Paul escapes by being let down in a basket from the wall. In Acts, however, the danger is said to come from the Jews, whereas in Paul's own account it comes from the governor of Damascus, *the*

commissioner of King Aretas of Arabia. Obviously we must prefer the first-hand story of what happened, but there may be some truth in the Acts narrative as well. It is possible that the Jews had intrigued with the authorities against Paul. In fact, the *commissioner* would be a Jew himself, and so may have been sympathetic towards the Jewish indignation at Paul's conversion. King Aretas is Aretas IV, King of the Nabataeans, who reigned from about A.D. 9 until A.D. 39. ✻

VISIONS AND REVELATIONS

12 I am obliged to boast. It does no good; but I shall go on **2** to tell of visions and revelations granted by the Lord. I know a Christian man who fourteen years ago (whether in the body or out of it, I do not know—God knows) was caught up as far as the third heaven. And I know that this **3** same man (whether in the body or out of it, I do not know—God knows) was caught up into paradise, and **4** heard words so secret that human lips may not repeat them. About such a man as that I am ready to boast; **5** but I will not boast on my own account, except of my weaknesses. If I should choose to boast, it would not be **6** the boast of a fool, for I should be speaking the truth. But I refrain, because I should not like anyone to form an estimate of me which goes beyond the evidence of his own eyes and ears. And so, to keep me from being **7** unduly elated by the magnificence of such revelations, I was given a sharp pain in my body which came as Satan's messenger to bruise me; this was to save me from being unduly elated. Three times I begged the Lord to **8** rid me of it, but his answer was: 'My grace is all you need; **9** power comes to its full strength in weakness.' I shall

therefore prefer to find my joy and pride in the very things that are my weakness; and then the power of Christ
10 will come and rest upon me. Hence I am well content, for Christ's sake, with weakness, contempt, persecution, hardship, and frustration; for when I am weak, then I am strong.

✲ Presumably the false apostles tried to impress people by boasting of the *visions* they had experienced. Paul feels bound to point out that he himself can do the same thing, if need be. Nevertheless, he is reticent in his description of what happened to him, and he knows that his experience must not be turned into a cause for personal pride. He looks upon the physical ailment from which he suffered as a warning against becoming *unduly elated*. The only legitimate ground for pride or for boasting, paradoxically enough, is the fact that one is compelled to undergo *weakness*, *contempt*, *persecution*, *hardship*, *and frustration*, since it is these experiences which provide scope for the exercise of the *power of Christ*.

2. Paul is obviously speaking of himself, although he says *a Christian man* and uses the third person in the following sentences. Perhaps he does so because he still finds it difficult to believe that such a vision could have been granted to him, or perhaps it occurred so far back in the past that it seems as though it had happened to a different person.

2–4. It is generally agreed that verse 2 and verses 3–4 describe the same experience, not two different visions. The expression *the third heaven* means the same thing to Paul as *paradise*. Opinions about *the third heaven* vary. It may signify the highest heaven of all, in other words the immediate neighbourhood of God himself. But this depends on how many heavens there were thought to be. Seven was a popular idea, and in that case transportation to the third one would not imply a very close approach to the presence of God. In this instance, however, it is the same as *paradise*, and paradise is spoken of as the abode of God in the Greek versions of Ezekiel (Ezek. 28: 13; 31: 8). It was thought of by the Jews as the region where the blessed, after death, go to dwell with God until the final resurrection. In any case the basic idea seems to be that Paul supposed himself to have experienced a state in which he felt very much nearer to the direct presence of God than he was during his normal, everyday existence.

The details of the experience are less clear to him. He does not know whether he was *in the body or out of it.* But he does give the impression that he intends his phrase *caught up* to be taken quite literally. He supposes either that he was transported bodily, upwards from earth to a heaven geographically located in outer space, or else that his soul was separated from his body, and likewise proceeded geographically upwards to the same heavenly region, thought of as existing in a spatial sense. If we ourselves fail to share his belief in the possibility of all this, are we to dismiss his experience as sheer imagination? Not necessarily. We might attempt to explain it in the following way. First of all, it is worth pointing out that a vision can be considered as a psychological condition brought about by God. It need not be thought of as a mere hallucination, a purely human product of mental disturbance. The Old Testament prophets saw visions, as well as 'hearing' God's Word in the sense of becoming inwardly conscious in their own minds of what the will of God was. If we believe that God directed their rational processes of thought and so used their conscious minds as a means of communicating with the rest of the nation, we can also believe that he directed the unconscious processes from which visions arise and equally made use of visionary experiences as a means of communicating some aspect of truth and some kind of knowledge of himself. Secondly, a vision can include other physical sensations as well as that of sight. Ezekiel felt himself to be transported by the hair of his head from Babylon to Jerusalem (Ezek. 8: 3). Paul, therefore, might well have experienced the bodily sensation of being carried from one place to another. But if this sensation was absent, and yet he seemed to find himself in a region apart from the earth, he might have felt that his body had been left behind. Thirdly, we might ourselves account for this particular event as follows. While he still remained on earth he underwent a visionary experience brought about by divine agency in which God was more directly present and in which a whole new dimension of existence was revealed to him. He was not transported from earth to heaven. Rather, the quality of life 'in heaven', i.e. life in the presence of God, became a momentary reality for him in an ecstatic condition which he experienced while here on earth. When he speaks of hearing *words so secret that human lips may not repeat them*, he is possibly referring to the praises offered to God by the inhabitants of heaven.

7. It is completely impossible to identify the physical disorder from which Paul suffered. Almost every disease in the medical dictionary has been suggested by one scholar and scorned by another. The more plausible suggestions include some kind of a recurrent fever and a form of eye trouble. This second idea is based on Gal. 4: 13–15, where Paul refers to his illness at the time of his first visit to the Galatians and also remarks that their affection for him was so great that they would have been willing to give him their very eyes. The illness is described here as *Satan's messenger*. For the notion of Satan's power to inflict physical suffering, see 1 Cor. 5: 5. In this instance, as in the Book of Job, he exercises this power with God's permission.

8. This is the only explicit example in the New Testament of prayer made directly to Christ (rather than to God). It is of considerable importance, as it shows that Paul thought of Christ as able to perform the functions of God (cf. 1 Cor. 8: 6). ✳

PAUL AND THE CONGREGATION AT CORINTH

I am being very foolish, but it was you who drove me to 11
it; my credentials should have come from you. In no
respect did I fall short of these superlative apostles, even
if I am a nobody. The marks of a true apostle were 12
there, in the work I did among you, which called for such
constant fortitude, and was attended by signs, marvels,
and miracles. Is there anything in which you were treated 13
worse than the other congregations—except this, that I
never sponged upon you? How unfair of me! I crave
forgiveness.

Here am I preparing to pay you a third visit; and I am 14
not going to sponge upon you. It is you I want, not
your money; parents should make provision for their
children, not children for their parents. As for me, I will 15
gladly spend what I have for you—yes, and spend myself
to the limit. If I love you overmuch, am I to be loved the
less? But, granted that I did not prove a burden to you, 16
still I was unscrupulous enough, you say, to use a trick to
catch you. Who, of the men I have sent to you, was used 17
by me to defraud you? I begged Titus to visit you, and I 18
sent our friend with him. Did Titus defraud you? Have
we not both been guided by the same Spirit, and followed
the same course?

✻ It should have been obvious to the Corinthians that Paul's
claim to be an apostle was genuine, and it was they who
should have defended him. His only failure to come up to their
expectations lay in his insistence upon remaining financially
independent of them. He explains that this was due to his own
affection for them. A parent delights to make provision for

his children and does not expect them, while they are still children, to make provision for him. Paul is the spiritual father of the Corinthian Christians and does not expect them to provide for his material support.

12. The *signs, marvels, and miracles* would include healings and exorcisms, possibly also the prediction of the future. It is worth noticing, however, that *the constant fortitude* displayed by the apostles is just as much an indication of their genuineness as are their more obviously unusual actions.

16–18. See 8: 16 — 9: 5. This is obviously a visit which has already taken place. Is it to be identified with the one mentioned in chapter 8 as about to happen? The general circumstances are similar. If the two visits are identical, we shall have to suppose that there has been some delay in the composition of the later paragraphs of the letter, so that there has been time for the visit to take place and for the Corinthians' reaction to Titus and his companions to become known to Paul. If this seems unlikely, and also if we think that chapters 10–13 of our present 2 Corinthians are part of a letter written before the one comprising chapters 1–9, we are forced to conclude that the writer is referring to some earlier visit to Corinth made by Titus, perhaps to the one hinted at in 8: 6 where the suggestion seems to be that it was Titus who actually began to make the first arrangements for the collection sometime during the previous year. ✻

FINAL REMARKS

19 Perhaps you think that all this time we have been addressing our defence to you. No; we are speaking in God's sight, and as Christian men. Our whole aim, my
20 own dear people, is to build you up. I fear that when I come I may perhaps find you different from what I wish you to be, and that you may find me also different from what you wish. I fear I may find quarrelling and jealousy,

angry tempers and personal rivalries, backbiting and gossip, arrogance and general disorder. I am afraid that, 21 when I come again, my God may humiliate me in your presence, that I may have tears to shed over many of those who have sinned in the past and have not repented of their unclean lives, their fornication and sensuality.

This will be my third visit to you; and all facts must be **13** established by the evidence of two or three witnesses. To those who have sinned in the past, and to everyone 2 else, I repeat the warning I gave before; I gave it in person on my second visit, and I give it now in absence. It is that when I come this time, I will show no leniency. Then you will have the proof you seek of the Christ who 3 speaks through me, the Christ who, far from being weak with you, makes his power felt among you. True, he 4 died on the cross in weakness, but he lives by the power of God; and we who share his weakness shall by the power of God live with him in your service.

Examine yourselves: are you living the life of faith? 5 Put yourselves to the test. Surely you recognize that Jesus Christ is among you?—unless of course you prove unequal to the test. I hope you will come to see that we 6 are not unequal to it. Our prayer to God is that we 7 may not have to hurt you; we are not concerned to be vindicated ourselves; we want you to do what is right, even if we should seem to be discredited. For we have no 8 power to act against the truth, but only for it. We are 9 well content to be weak at any time if only you are strong. Indeed, my whole prayer is that all may be put right with you. My purpose in writing this letter before 10 I come, is to spare myself, when I come, any sharp exercise of authority—authority which the Lord gave me for building up and not for pulling down.

11 And now, my friends, farewell. Mend your ways; take our appeal to heart; agree with one another; live in peace;
12 and the God of love and peace will be with you. Greet
13 one another with the kiss of peace. All God's people send you greetings.

14 The grace of the Lord Jesus Christ, and the love of God, and fellowship in the Holy Spirit, be with you all.

✻ Paul warns the congregation that he is about to visit Corinth for the third time. They must improve their attitude and their general conduct before he arrives, lest he should be compelled to take stern action. It is their own welfare he is concerned for.

12: 21. When he says that he is afraid lest God should *humiliate* him he does not mean that he will fail to take de-cisive action (and so justify his opponents' accusation of weak-ness of character), but simply that he will feel bitterly ashamed of his converts' behaviour unless they mend their ways.

13: 1. See Deut. 19: 15. The same rule is alluded to in Matt. 18: 16.

3–4. Paul's readers have implicitly accused him of *weakness*. He reminds them that although sharing in the experiences of Christ may involve sharing his experience of human weakness, nevertheless it also means having a share in the divine power which belongs to Christ. The Corinthians take this for granted in their own case (cf. 1 Cor. 4: 8–10), but they forget that it must be true of Paul as well.

5. The recognition that *Jesus Christ is among* the members of the church should lead to the complete avoidance of the ill-conduct of which Paul complains (cf. 1 Cor. 6: 15–17). If they *prove unequal to the test,* that is, if their ill-conduct persists, then they are not *living the life of faith* and presumably must expect Christ to withdraw his presence from them.

14. Paul is not here presenting us with any formal doctrine of the Trinity. He nowhere gives explicit attention to the precise nature of the relationship between Christ, God, and the Spirit. The prayer that the *grace of the Lord Jesus Christ* may be with his readers is a prayer that Christ may continue to show himself gracious towards them, and that they may be spiritually enriched as a result of his original and supreme act of gracious generosity in becoming man (8: 9). The *love of God* needs no comment, except that it has been especially revealed in God's giving of his Son to die for the human race (Rom. 5: 8; 8: 32). This phrase, therefore, means much the same as the preceding one. The prayer for *fellowship in the Holy Spirit* is a petition that the Corinthians may share in the divine power of the Spirit and also that they may experience among themselves the mutual love which the Spirit creates within the Christian community. ✻

✻   ✻   ✻   ✻   ✻   ✻   ✻   ✻   ✻   ✻   ✻   ✻   ✻

THE CORINTHIAN LETTERS TODAY

The reactions of the modern reader to the Corinthian letters are likely to be somewhat mixed. Sometimes we are on familiar ground, because the problems Paul deals with are similar to our own. The church in Corinth was disunited, just as the whole Church is today. Wherever we live in the English-speaking countries, we may be sure that somewhere in the neighbourhood there will be a Roman Catholic church, a Methodist church, an Anglican or Episcopalian church, and possibly Lutherans, Congregationalists, Baptists, and Presbyterians as well. Paul's answer to the disunity in Corinth is that exaggerated loyalty to one particular apostle detracts from loyalty to Christ. In the same way, the members of the different denominations today have realized that their lack of unity is a serious hindrance to the effective presentation of the Christian faith to non-Christians. To convince the rest of the world that the nature of God himself is revealed in the personality and activity of Jesus is much more important for Christians than to spend their time and energy in arguing whether one form of church organization or worship is superior to another.

Strange ideas in the Corinthian correspondence

In other respects, however, the ideas expressed in these two letters are entirely foreign to our own ways of thought. This element of strangeness is not confined to the Corinthian correspondence: it appears in the rest of the New Testament as well. It is a difficulty which cannot be overcome merely by producing a more modern and idiomatic translation. However clear the translation may be, it cannot dispose of the strange ideas. When the New English Bible was first published, one of my pupils was most disappointed to discover that the translators had failed to remove from the Gospels all the references to evil spirits. They should have done so, she maintained, because we ourselves no longer believe in the existence of such beings. But a translator must translate what is there in the text before him. He is not at liberty to leave out the notions he disapproves of. Paul's correspondence is full of ideas now strange to us. He shared the Gospel writers' belief in evil spiritual powers. He believed that Christ would shortly return to the earth in glory. He spoke of Christians as included within the personality of Christ. We find all this in the Corinthian letters. From our own point of view it is very odd indeed. Does it mean anything at all?

Do the strange ideas matter?

Before we attempt an answer there is a preliminary question to be dealt with. Does it matter whether or not these strange ideas mean anything to us? If an examination candidate can give a sufficiently accurate account of them to satisfy the examiners, why should he or she need to bother about them any further? (In other words, why am I writing this concluding essay instead of leaving the preceding commentary to speak for itself?) I would suggest that the need for further discussion arises for the following reason. Very few people study a subject simply and solely for examination results. Most of them begin the course, at least, as a result of some genuine interest in it. And a serious interest in any department of learning means that the student both desires and expects to achieve a greater understanding of some aspect of truth, whether it be the truth about the physical universe, or the truth about human nature, or the truth about past events. The student of religion, in particular, is concerned to learn something more of the truth about the existence and nature of God and about the underlying purpose of human life. Now the writers of the New Testament claim that the truth about God and the truth about man was revealed to them by Jesus of Nazareth. His life showed them what the character of God is like. He demonstrated to them, through his own words and actions, the perfect human personality and the ideal relationship between man and God. They claim that Jesus was sent from God. In the activity of Jesus we are to recognize the activity of God himself. For those students of the New Testament who accept these claims there is a further consequence. It is asserted that God chose to reveal the truth about himself at a particular point in history, i.e. the beginning of the first century A.D., and that he made this disclosure of his nature to a particular group of people, i.e. those Jews who became followers of Jesus. This group of people thought in a particular way: they believed in evil spirits and had some peculiar notion of corporate personality. Now if God chose to make himself fully understood, for the first time in human history, to people who thought like this, then the conclusion follows that there must be some truth, some meaning, in their ways of thought, however strange they may seem to us. We cannot, therefore, discard them as meaningless. If we are unable to accept them as they stand, we are bound to try to reinterpret them, and to make some sense out of them so that they may be applied to our own situation in the twentieth century.

Corporate personality: Adam and Christ

Perhaps the most difficult idea we have met with in the interpretation of the Corinthian letters is the use of the Jewish concept of corporate personality to explain the relationship between Christ and his followers. A group of people is thought of as a single personal unit, and the action of one representative member of the group is the action of all the members: 'one man died for all, and therefore all mankind has died'. Adam contained within his body the whole human race of which he was the ancestor, and all men share his disobedient and rebellious attitude towards God. Christ also is an inclusive personality, and all men may share his love for God.

Difficulties of this way of thinking

Why, exactly, do we find this difficult? It might seem that the idea of representative action is, after all, a quite common one in everyday human affairs. We often find individuals acting on behalf of groups. A trade union official may ask for a wage increase. If the employers grant the request, it is all the workers in their business whose pay rises, not only the pay of the man who put their case forward. But when we look at what Paul says about Christ we are confronted with three questions which do not occur in connexion with the kind of incident we have just considered. First, how can one human being change the relationship of another human being to God? Surely this is a matter of individual responsibility. We cannot believe in God on behalf of someone else. The decision to believe or not to believe is one which each person has to make for himself. Secondly, how can one human being act on behalf of the whole human race? Thirdly, how can the action of one man in the past directly affect the nature and destiny of people living many hundreds of years after? The Jews of Paul's day, and Paul himself, believed that Adam had in fact done all this. A single individual, he was at the same time the ancestor of all humanity, and this explained the far-reaching consequences of his action. Accepting this, Paul could then pass naturally on to the thought that the one man Christ, whom he saw as the creator of a new kind of humanity, had likewise so acted as to involve all other men in the consequences of his action. But if we do not ourselves share the Jewish beliefs about Adam, the awkward questions remain.

Again, we can readily see that there is some truth in the concept of corporate personality in the sense that each of us as an individual is affected by the values and conduct of the society in which we live. We are not completely isolated and individually independent. If all our friends and acquaintances think that what matters most is to make a lot of money as quickly as possible, we ourselves are likely to think the same. If everyone else goes in for status symbols such as expensive cameras and powerful cars, we want them as well. If a boy falls in with a gang of youths who think that it is clever to steal if you can get away with it, he is likely eventually to adopt the same attitude himself. If a social group is morally corrupt, it is probable that those who are born into it will become morally corrupt as well. This is part of the meaning of the Adam myth. Adam stands for our ancestors and our contemporaries, for the whole human race which is to some extent corrupted by evil. Because we are born as members of the human race we become corrupted as well. In that sense we are affected by the sin of Adam. We follow the example set us by the society in which we grow up. If this is what Adam means, then we might suppose that it is comparatively easy to understand in a similar way what Paul says about Christ. The followers of Christ were affected by the example he set of love for God and obedience to God. The members of the Church in the succeeding generation were affected by their example, and so on. Children born of Christian parents are born into a social group which believes in God and tries to obey him, and so they grow up with a similar attitude.

All this is true, but it is not the whole truth, either of what the Jews believed about Adam or of what Paul believed about Christ. It is more than a matter of setting a human example. Take first the Jewish belief about Adam. Adam did not only set his descendants an example of sinful conduct. He actually passed on to them his own sinful nature. Perhaps we could illustrate the difference in the following way, transferring the idea from the spiritual and moral sphere to the physical. A man may set an example of physical fitness to others by taking exercise and following a sensible diet. But in the case of his own children it may not only be a question of setting them an example. He may perhaps have actually passed on to them his own physical characteristics and his own healthy constitution. What the Jews believed about Adam, Paul believed about Christ. He did not merely set his followers an example. He passed on to them his own personality.

It is difficult for us, however, to think as the Jews thought about Adam. We cannot, in any case, believe that Adam was a single historical individual from whom all mankind is descended, and this means that the example of Adam loses for us the comparative simplicity and clarity it possessed for Paul. But even if we could believe this, we should, I think, find it even more difficult to believe, as the Jews did, that Adam passed on to his descendants an evil moral and spiritual nature simply by means of physical transmission. The process of physical reproduction may involve the transmission of physical characteristics from parent to offspring. We should not ourselves think it likely that an attitude of disobedience to God could be passed on in this way. So we are once more confronted with the question, if we cannot think as Paul thought about Adam, can we still think as he did about Christ? Before we consider this question, however, it may be worth noticing that even in Paul's case what he has to say about Adam is more of an illustration than an explanation of what he says about Christ. The followers of Christ are not related to him physically in the way that Paul supposed the human race to be physically related to Adam. The parallel he draws between Adam and Christ shows us what he wants to say about the meaning of Christ's action but does not explain exactly why this action should have the significance he attributes to it.

We are left, then, with these questions. How are we to explain the belief that Christ changes our own individual relationship to God? How are we to explain Paul's conviction that what happened to Christ happened to us, that Christ communicates his personality to his followers, and that they are 'in Christ', i.e. included within his own personal life? The following line of thought is merely an attempt at solving a very difficult problem. The beginning of the argument may seem a little remote from the point at issue, but its relevance will become apparent as the discussion continues.

Man's personal relationship to God dependent upon Christ

If we believe in God, we believe that it is from God that the whole universe derives its existence. We ourselves are alive only because the living God exists and has given life to us. If God did not exist, we should not exist either. In 1 Cor. 8: 6 Paul says: 'there is one God, the Father, from whom all being comes'. In Acts, our dependence upon God for life is described as living 'in' him: 'for in him we live and move, in him we exist' (Acts 17: 28). Furthermore, in the same sentence in 1 Corinthians, Paul goes on to speak of God as the one 'towards whom we move'. In other words, we are created for a personal relationship with God. We are capable of loving God, in response to his own love for us, demonstrated in the very fact that he has brought us into existence. Now if it is true that we derive our whole existence from God, we must also believe that we derive from him our capacity for responsive love. If we live only because God has life in himself and conveys life to us, we must possess the capacity for responsive love only because this kind of love is an aspect of the nature of God himself, and a personal quality which is communicated to us by God. This aspect of the being of God is revealed to us within our own human situation by Christ. The writer of the Gospel according to John strongly emphasizes the responsive and loving obedience of the Son to the Father, and makes it very clear that this personal relationship which we see in action upon the plane of human history is an illustration of the relationship of Son to Father within the eternal being of God. We can therefore say that it is because God exists, in one mode of his being, as God the Son, that we ourselves can exist as beings created for a responsive relationship of love towards God. It is therefore from Christ that we derive our real personality. We could say that as persons we exist 'in Christ', just as the author of Acts expresses the belief that we derive our life in general from God by saying that 'in him we live'. Our personal relationship with God is possible only because, in our limited and human fashion, we are able to share in the eternal and infinite responsive love of the Son for the Father. Our relationship with God is derived from and depends upon the relationship of Christ to God.

It is nevertheless a relationship which we are free to break up and discontinue if we choose. A man is free to refuse God's gift of life by committing suicide. He can likewise refuse to share the love and obedience of the Son and so become hostile to God or disregard his existence. According to the New Testament writers, this is what actually happens in the case of every single member of the whole human race. The whole of mankind is estranged from God. If the personal relationship between God and man is to be repaired, a process of reconciliation becomes necessary.

Reconciliation of man to God through Christ

Now we have argued already that man's relationship to God is possible at all only in so far as it depends upon Christ's prior relationship to him. Therefore, if man is to be reconciled to God, the Son himself must experience man's state of estrangement, and deal with it and overcome it through his own love for the Father. This is what we see happening in the life, death and resurrection of Jesus. Jesus finds himself in a situation where he knows what it is like to be tempted to disobey God and go his own way. He feels himself cut off from personal contact with God, and as he is dying he cries out: 'My God, my God, why hast thou forsaken me?' (Mark 15: 34). His death itself, according to Paul, is the acceptance of the consequences of man's sin, i.e. of man's alienation from God. But just as during his earthly life Jesus continually overcame the temptation to disobedience, so also the New Testament writers maintain that he overcame death as well. He was restored to life, and exalted to the right hand of God in heaven. The Fourth Gospel speaks of him as going to the Father. His experience of estrangement was over, and his communion with the Father in love is unqualified and absolute. Nevertheless, since the experience of estrangement was a reality, this relationship now possesses an aspect which might be described as the experience of reconciliation. It is love which has overcome a tendency towards alienation. Therefore the reconciliation of men to God becomes a real possibility. In that sense, Christ has changed our relationship to God. What happened to him happened, potentially, to all of us, because it is his own relationship to the Father which makes ours possible. His experience of reconciliation may become ours. In that sense he communicates his personal life to us, and we share in his personality.

Again, we can choose to do so or not. As individuals we are free to opt out of the situation created for us by the death and resurrection of Christ. We may choose not to take advantage of it. But if we do choose to take advantage of it, if we accept the Christian faith and become members of the Church, then as individuals we are included within the personal life of Christ. We are 'in Christ', to use Paul's phrase, and share his relationship to God.

Christ and the Church

If we go on to ask precisely how the personal life of Christ is communicated to his followers, we are bound to admit that this is ultimately a mystery of which no complete explanation can be given within the limitations of human thought. To take up the illustration which we have used in the previous stages of the argument, we cannot ultimately explain how God communicates life to the universe as a whole. How is it that anything exists at all? How is it that the universe continues in being, instead of disintegrating into nothingness? These are questions to which we have no answer. Similarly, we cannot explain how God the Son communicates to man his own personal character of responsive love. But we do know that we are alive and that the universe exists, even though we are unable to say how. Likewise, the first Christians knew that the members of the Church shared the personal character of Christ. They saw in each other the qualities which they knew Jesus to have possessed: love, kindness, goodness and gentleness. They were conscious of being motivated and empowered by a personal force beyond themselves, and since the results were manifestly good, they spoke of this power as the Spirit of Christ, or as the Spirit of God, made available to them by Christ. Their daily experience attested the reality of their beliefs about the relationship between Christ and his followers, despite the inadequacy of the explanation which they (or we) might give of it.

The return of Christ and the invisible powers

It remains to consider more briefly the two other ideas which we mentioned as strange and unfamiliar to us: Paul's belief that Christ would shortly return in glory to the earth, and his belief in the existence of invisible powers, for the most part evil, which were able to influence human life.

His expectation that Christ would return to earth in the very near future and bring to an end human history as we know it was plainly mistaken. It is now some nineteen hundred years after Paul's death. The present world continues to exist, and no such event as the one he hoped for has taken place. Has his expectation no further meaning? Was it just a mistake, and is that all there is to be said? Perhaps not quite all. The meaning of Christ's coming, or part of the meaning, was that it would mark the final destruction of all the evil that there is in the universe. It would be the end not only of human wickedness but also of all the evil in the natural world—pain, decay, and death. Paul believed so strongly and confidently that evil would eventually be overcome and abolished that it seemed to him that this must happen very soon. His expectation of the immediate return of Christ is no good to us if we regard it merely as a timetable of events which proved incorrect. But if we think of it as expressing the intensity of his conviction that evil can be overcome, and that pain, suffering, and wickedness are not the final answer to the question of what human life is like, then it may hold some meaning for us who live in the twentieth century just as much as it did for him in the first century.

This takes us some way also towards explaining the significance of Paul's belief in evil spiritual powers. He was not interested in these powers in themselves. This is perhaps shown by the fact that he nowhere makes it clear what their nature precisely was. He was interested only because he believed that they had been deprived of their power by Christ. And Christ's victory over them is a further symbolic picture, illustrating the conviction that the Christian faith provides a practical answer to the problem of evil, whether or not we can completely account for its origin. But there may be a little more to be said here. Both Greeks and Jews thought that the invisible powers were connected with natural phenomena. They ruled the planets, and controlled the winds and the rain and the seas. Now as long as it was generally believed that the processes of nature were controlled by these demonic forces, it was not possible for men to make much progress in understanding and controlling their natural environment. Christianity removed the fear of the demons, by insisting that they had been subdued by Christ. It therefore helped to make possible the rise of natural science. I quote from a modern philosopher: 'by clearing away all sorts of false and frightening views of the way the universe worked, Paul helped later generations to explore its secrets without fear of malign forces. And with confidence of success too: for its processes were no longer regarded as governed by their caprice' (D. M. MacKinnon, in *New Essays in Philosophical Theology*, p. 176). We might therefore say that the victory of Christ over the invisible powers is a reality for us, even though we might not believe in their existence as such.

This discussion of some of Paul's ideas is only a sample of the kind of thing that needs to be done when we study his letters. It is not intended as a complete elucidation of all the difficulties, but rather as a stimulus to encourage readers to think about the problems which arise and to discover other solutions and better explanations for themselves.

INDEX

Achaia, viii, 1, 117
Achan, 53–4, 90
Adam, 80, 108, 113–14, 186–9
Agabus, 97
ages
  The Age to Come, 25, 26
  This Age, 24–5, 26
angels, 43, 80, 92
animal body, 113
Antioch, viii, 3
Antiochus Epiphanes, 55, 93
Aphrodite, 48
Apocalypse of Baruch, 103–4
Apollos, 18, 19, 31, 35, 114, 117
apostles
  appearances of Jesus to, 104–5
  conduct of, 125, 138, 148–9, 154
  definition of, 15
  false apostles, 12, 119, 167, 169, 171–2
  hardships of their life, 36, 110, 140–1, 154
  privileges of, 66–7, 68–9
  signs of, 180
  work of, 33, 35, 129–30, 131, 135
Aquila, 2, 118
Aretas, 175
Athens, viii, 71, 151
authority, in divine and human relationships, 79–81

baptism, 19, 44, 73, 90
  for the dead, 109–10
Barnabas, 93, 105
Beroea, viii, 162
blasphemy, 86–7
Body of Christ, 16, 48, 85, 89–90, 92, 108, 114, 126, 145, 146, 147
body, physical, 46–7, 48, 49, 51–2, 146
  'give my body to be burnt', 93

celibacy, 58–9
  partners in, 59–60

Cephas (Peter), 18, 19, 31, 67, 104
Chloe, 11
Christ
  and the Spirit, 136–8
  divinity of, 16, 63–4, 73, 172, 178
  example of, 162
  'in Christ', 16, 37, 145, 147, 189, 190, 192
  kingdom of, 36
  obedience of, 125
  participation of the Christian in the personality and experiences of, 48, 122–3, 140–1, 145, 147, 149, 182, 186–92
  prayer to, 178
  relationship to God the Father, 79, 109, 190–1
  representative action of, 149, 152–3, 186, 187, 188–9, 191
  return of, 16, 103, 109, 115, 118, 143, 144, 184, 193
  see also Day of the Lord
Christ-party, 18–19
Church
  people of God (holy community), 15–16, 44, 53–4, 55, 156, 171
  temple of God (metaphor of the building), 32–3, 145, 157
  see also Body of Christ
circumcision, 55, 71, 161
Claudius, 2, 118
collection for the Jerusalem church, 5, 117, 160–1, 163–4, 165
conscience, 64–5, 138
Corinth, viii, 1–2
Corinthian letters
  date and place of composition, 10–13
  unity of 1 Corinthians, 3–5
  unity of 2 Corinthians, 5–10
corporate personality, 53–4, 90, 108, 145, 147, 184, 185, 186–92
covenant
  new, 84

covenant (*cont.*)
old and new, 132–3, 134–6
creation, 80, 139, 171
new creation, 139, 149, 171–2
Crete, viii, 129
Crispus, 2, 19

Damascus, viii, 174
Day of the Lord, 16–17, 32, 40
Day of Pentecost, 98
death, 107, 108, 109, 115, 132–3,
142–7
of Christ, 20–1, 23, 25–6, 41, 77,
84, 104, 149, 153, 183, 186, 191
dedication, 44
demonic powers, 48, 76–7, 184, 185,
193–4
dictation, 13, 118
Didache, 118
distribution of possessions, 93, 161
disunity, 11, 18–19, 29, 30, 83, 85,
183–4
divorce, 11, 52–3

ecstatic utterance, 92, 94, 97–100
ekklesia, 15–16
Ephesus, viii, 10, 11, 12, 13, 110, 119,
120
Epictetus, 89
Epicureans, 151
Eucharist (Lord's Supper), 73, 77,
82–5, 118, 128
Eve, 80
excommunication, 39–40, 128
Exodus, 22, 41, 73
exorcism, 180
Ezekiel, 177

faith, 87–8, 93–5
flesh, fleshly, 29–30, 157
forgiveness, 22, 25, 41, 44, 134
fornication, 2, 11, 45–9, 74
freedom, 45–6, 49, 56, 64–5, 66

Gaius, 19
Gallio, 2
Gentile Christians, 161
ghosts, 104, 143

glory, 26, 135–6, 137
glossa, 98
golden calf, 74
'governing powers', 25–6, 43, 139
grace, 16, 183

healing, 86, 87, 180
Heavenly Man, 114
holiness, holy, 16, 44
hope, 93–5

idol meat, 4, 11, 61–2, 64–5, 76–7, 157
idolatry, idols, 62, 74, 76
image of God, 79–80
incest, 11, 39–40
indiscipline, act of, 119–20, 127, 128
Israelites, 15–16, 72–4, 135

James, 67, 105
Jeremiah, 84, 132
Jerusalem church, 93, 105, 160–1, 165
Jesus
brothers of, 67
sayings of, 41, 43–4, 52, 69, 83,
88, 93, 122
Jewish beliefs and customs, 39–40,
41, 46–7, 52, 68, 69, 76, 89–90,
103–4, 108, 130, 143, 146, 185–8
Jewish Christians, 161, 167
judgement, 16–17, 21, 32, 36, 43,
44, 58
Justin, 118

kingdom of God, 16–17, 37–8, 40,
43, 44, 109
kiss of peace, 118

Law of Moses, 21, 39, 46, 67, 71, 132,
134–6, 161, 167, 174
lawsuits, 11, 43–4
letter, metaphor of the, 131
love, 62, 92, 93, 94
of Christ, 190–2
of God, 183, 189
Lystra, viii, 37, 71, 174

Macedonia, viii, 12, 13, 117, 120,
121, 125, 161, 162, 164

manna, 73, 162
Marana tha, 118
marriage, 11, 51–4
  to unbelievers, 156–7
martyrdom, 93
Menander, 110
Messiah, 109, 126, 149–50
Moses, 73, 74, 135–6

'nakedness' (disembodiment), 143–6
name of Jesus, 16, 40, 44
Nero, 93

Onesimus, 56

pagan gods, 62, 87
pagans, avoidance of contact with,
  41–2, 155–7
paidagogos, 37
'painful letter', 3, 7, 12, 13, 127, 159
paradise, 176–7
Passover, 41
Paul
  apostolic vocation of, 69–70
  appearance of, 23
  conversion of, 105
  correspondence with the Corin-
    thians, 3–13
  defence of his apostolic authority
    and conduct, 4, 15, 66–7, 124–5,
    131, 167–8, 169, 182
  disease from which he suffered, 23,
    123, 178
  hardships of his life as an apostle,
    174–5
  mission to the Gentiles, 169
  opposition to, 119–20, 128, 174–5
  renunciation of apostolic privileges
    of, 68–70, 172, 179–80
  rights as a Roman citizen, 174
  vision of, 176–8
  visits to Corinth, 1–2, 11, 119–21,
    182
period before the return of Christ,
  58–9, 92
Pharaoh, 73
Philemon, 56
Philippi, viii, 162, 174

Philo of Alexandria, 114
pillar of cloud, 73
Plato, 103
Pontius Pilate, 26
prayer, 80–1, 98, 99, 125
preaching of the Gospel, 20, 21, 69–
  70, 130
'previous letter', 3, 8, 12, 13, 41–2,
  53, 119–20, 156
Prisca (Priscilla), 2, 118
prophecy, Christian, 80–1, 86, 94,
  97, 99–100, 102
  fulfilment of O.T. prophecy, 74,
    125
prophetic symbolism, 84
prophets, O.T., 17, 177
prostitutes, sacred, 48

rebirth, 37
reconciliation, 22, 150–3, 191–2
redemption, 22
resurrection, 11, 26–7, 47, 59, 94–5,
  103–15, 143, 144, 147, 177
  of Jesus, 41, 63, 67, 79, 104–5, 107,
    108, 109, 114, 123, 191
resurrection body, 112–15, 143, 144,
  145, 146, 147
righteousness, 21
rock, supernatural, 73
Rome, viii, 169

sacrifice, 61, 62, 76–7
Sadducees, 104
Satan (Belial), 40, 128, 129, 139, 157,
  172, 178
Scripture, fulfilment of, 104
Septuagint, 15–16
sexual abstinence, 51–2
sexual intercourse, 46, 48, 52
Sinai, 135
slavery, 55–6, 93
social distinctions, 2, 83
Socrates, 21
Sosthenes, 15
soul, immortal, 46, 47, 51–2, 103,
  143
Spain, 169
spirit, 27, 157

INDEX

Spirit of God (Holy Spirit, Spirit of Christ), 27–8, 29–30, 33, 38, 44, 49, 64, 80, 86, 87, 90, 92, 97, 99, 113, 126, 131–3, 134, 136–7, 139, 148, 183, 192

spiritual body, 113

spiritual gifts, 11, 36, 86–8, 91, 92, 94, 97–100

Stephanas, 19, 118

Stoicism, 89

sufferings
  of Christ, 122–3
  of Christians, 122–3

Tacitus, 93

Thessalonica, viii, 162

third heaven, 176–7

Timothy, 37, 71, 117, 120

Titus, 7, 120, 129, 161, 163–4, 180

Trinity, doctrine of the, 63–4, 183

Troas, viii, 120

unbelief, 138–9

veil, allegory of the, 135–6

weak, the, 64–5, 71

wisdom
  Christian, 24, 26–7
  divine, 20–1
  human (worldly), 19, 21, 23, 33, 168

women
  silent in the assembly, 102
  subordination of, 78–81
  veiling of, 78–9, 80–1

worship, public, 11, 78, 80–1, 97–100, 101–2